A Noble Life

Dinah Maria Mulock Craik

BIBLIOLIFE

A NOBLE LIFE.

BY

THE AUTHOR OF

"JOHN HALIFAX, GENTLEMAN,"
"CHRISTIAN'S MISTAKE,"
&c.. &c., &c.

FIAT VOLUNTAS TUA.

NEW YORK:
HARPER & BROTHERS, PUBLISHERS,
FRANKLIN SQUARE.
1871.

Dedicated.

WITH THE AFFECTION OF EIGHTEEN YEARS,

TO

UNCLE GEORGE.

A Noble Life.

Chapter the First.

MANY years ago, how many need not be recorded, there lived in his ancestral castle, in the far north of Scotland, the last Earl of Cairnforth.

You will not find his name in "Lodge's Peerage," for, as I say, he was the last earl, and with him the title became extinct. It had been borne for centuries by many noble and gallant men, who had lived worthily or died bravely. But I think among what we call "heroic" lives —lives the story of which touches us with something higher than pity, and deeper than love—there never was any of his race who left behind a history more truly heroic than he.

Now that it is all over and done—now that the soul so mysteriously given has gone back unto Him who gave it, and a little green turf in the kirk-yard behind Cairnforth Manse covers the poor body in which it dwelt for more than forty years, I feel it might do good to many, and would do harm to none, if I related the story—a very simple one, and more like a biography than a tale —of Charles Edward Stuart Montgomerie, last Earl of Cairnforth.

He did not succeed to the title; he was born Earl of Cairnforth, his father having been drowned in the loch a month before, the wretched countess herself beholding the sight from her castle windows. She lived but to know she had a son and heir — to whom she desired might be given his father's name: then she died—more glad than sorry to depart, for she had loved her husband all her life, and had only been married to him a year. Perhaps, had she once seen her son, she might have wished less to die than to live, if only for his sake; however, it was not God's will that this should be. So, at two days old, the "poor little earl"—as from his very birth people began compassionately to call him—was left alone in the world, without a single near relative or connection, his parents having both been only children, but with his title, his estate, and twenty thousand a year.

Cairnforth Castle is one of the loveliest residences in all Scotland. It is built on the extremity of a long tongue of land which stretches out between two salt-water lochs—Loch Beg, the "little," and Loch Mhor, the "big" lake. The latter is grand and gloomy, shut in by bleak mountains, which sit all round it, their feet in the water, and their heads in mist and cloud. But Loch Beg is quite different. It has green, cultivated, sloping shores, fringed with trees to the water's edge, and the least ray of sunshine seems always to set it dimpling with wavy smiles. Now and then a sudden squall comes down from the chain of mountains far away beyond the head of the loch, and then its waters begin to darken—just like a sudden frown over a bright face; the waves curl and rise, and lash themselves into foam, and any little sailing boat, which has been happily and safely riding over them five minutes before, is often struck and capsized immediately. Thus it happened when the late earl was drowned.

The minister — the Rev. Alexander Cardross — had

been out sailing with him; had only just landed, and was watching the boat crossing back again, when the squall came down. Though this region is a populous district now, with white villas dotted like daisies all along the green shores, there was then not a house in the whole peninsula of Cairnforth except the Castle, the Manse, and a few cottages, called the "clachan." Before help was possible, the earl and his boatman, Neil Campbell, were both drowned. The only person saved was little Malcolm Campbell—Neil's brother—a boy about ten years old.

In most country parishes of Scotland or England there is an almost superstitious feeling that "the minister," or "the clergyman," must be the fittest person to break any terrible tidings. So it ought to be. Who but the messenger of God should know best how to communicate His awful will, as expressed in great visitations of calamity? In this case no one could have been more suited for his solemn office than Mr. Cardross. He went up to the Castle door, as he had done to that of many a cottage, bearing the same solemn message of sudden death, to which there could be but one answer — "Thy will be done."

But the particulars of that terrible interview, in which he had to tell the countess what already her own eyes had witnessed—though they refused to believe the truth —the minister never repeated to any creature except his wife. And afterward, during the four weeks that Lady Cairnforth survived her husband, he was the only person, beyond her necessary attendants, who saw her until she died.

A 2

The day after her death he was suddenly summoned to the castle by Mr. Menteith, an Edinburg writer to the signet, and confidential agent, or factor, as the office is called in Scotland, to the late earl.

"They'll be sending for you to baptize the child. It's early—but the puir bit thing may be delicate, and they may want it done at once, before Mr. Menteith returns to Edinburg."

"Maybe so, Helen; so do not expect me back till you see me."

Thus saying, the minister quitted his sunshiny manse garden, where he was working peacefully among his raspberry-bushes, with his wife looking on, and walked, in meditative mood, through the Cairnforth woods, now blue with hyacinths in their bosky shadows, and in every nook and corner starred with great clusters of yellow primroses, which in this part of the country grow profusely, even down to within a few feet of high-water mark, on the tidal shores of the lochs. Their large, round, smiling faces, so irresistibly suggestive of baby smiles at sight of them, and baby fingers clutching at them, touched the heart of the good minister, who had left two small creatures of his own—a "bit girlie" of five, and a two-year-old boy—playing on his grass-plot at home with some toys of the countess's giving: she had always been exceedingly kind to the Manse children.

He thought of her, lying dead; and then of her poor little motherless and fatherless baby, whom, if she had any consciousness in her death-hour, it must have been a sore pang to her to leave behind. And the tears gathered again and again in the good man's eyes, shutting out from his vision all the beauty of the spring.

He reached the grand Italian portico, built by some former earl with a taste for that style, and yet harmonizing well with the smooth lawn, bounded by a circle of magnificent trees, through which came glimpses of the glittering loch. The great doors used almost always to stand open, and the windows were rarely closed — the countess liked sunshine and fresh air, but now all was shut up and silent, and not a soul was to be seen about the place.

Mr. Cardross sighed, and walked round to the other side of the castle, where was my lady's flower-garden, or what was to be made into one. Then he entered by French windows, from a terrace overlooking it, my lord's library, also incomplete. For the earl, who was by no means a bookish man, had only built that room since his marriage, to please his wife, whom perhaps he loved all the better that she was so exceedingly unlike himself. Now both were away—their short dream of married life ended, their plans and hopes crumbled into dust. As yet, no external changes had been made, the other solemn changes having come so suddenly. Gardeners still worked in the parterres, and masons and carpenters still, in a quiet and lazy manner, went on completing the beautiful room; but there was no one to order them—no one watched their work. Except for workmen, the place seemed so deserted that Mr. Cardross wandered through the house for some time before he found a single servant to direct him to the person of whom he was in search.

Mr. Menteith sat alone in a little room filled with guns and fishing-rods, and ornamented with stag's heads, stuffed birds, and hunting relics of all sorts, which had been called, not too appropriately, the earl's "study." He was a little, dried-up man, about fifty years old, of sharp but not unkindly aspect. When the minister entered, he looked up from the mass of papers which he seemed to have been trying to reduce into some kind of order—apparently the late earl's private papers, which had been untouched since his death, for there was a sad and serious shadow over what would otherwise have been rather a humorous face.

"Welcome, Mr. Cardross; I am indeed glad to see you. I took the liberty of sending for you, since you are the only person with whom I can consult—we can consult, I should say, for Dr. Hamilton wished it likewise—on this —this most painful occasion."

"I shall be very glad to be of the slightest service," returned Mr. Cardross. "I had the utmost respect for those that are away." He had a habit, this tender-hearted, pious man, who, with all his learning, kept a religious faith as simple as a child's, of always speaking of the dead as only "away."

The two gentlemen sat down together. They had often met before, for whenever there were guests at Cairnforth Castle the earl always invited the minister and his wife to dinner, but they had never fraternized much. Now, a common sympathy, nay, more, a common grief —for something beyond sympathy, keen personal regret, was evidently felt by both for the departed earl and countess—made them suddenly familiar.

"Is the child doing well?" was Mr. Cardross's first and most natural question; but it seemed to puzzle Mr. Menteith exceedingly.

"I suppose so — indeed, I can hardly say. This is a most difficult and painful matter."

"It was born alive, and is a son and heir, as I heard?"

"Yes."

"That is fortunate."

"For some things; since, had it been a girl, the title would have lapsed, and the long line of Earls of Cairn-forth ended. At one time Dr. Hamilton feared the child would be stillborn, and then, of course, the earldom would have been extinct. The property must in that case have passed to the earl's distant cousins, the Bruces, of whom you may have heard, Mr. Cardross?"

"I have; and there are few things, I fancy, which Lord Cairnforth would have regretted more than such heir-ship."

"You are right," said the keen W. S., evidently re-lieved. "It was my instinctive conviction that you were in the late earl's confidence on this point, which made me decide to send and consult with you. We must take all precautions, you see. We are placed in a most painful and responsible position—both Dr. Hamilton and myself."

It was now Mr. Cardross's turn to look perplexed. No doubt it was a most sad fatality which had happened, but still things did not seem to warrant the excessive anxiety testified by Mr. Menteith.

"I do not quite comprehend you. There might have been difficulties as to the succession, but are they not all solved by the birth of a healthy, living heir—whom we must cordially hope will long continue to live?"

"I hardly know if we ought to hope it," said the law-yer, very seriously. "But we must 'keep a calm sough'" on that matter for the present—so far, at least, Dr. Hamilton and I have determined — in order to prevent the Bruces from getting wind of it. Now, then, will you come and see the earl?"

"The earl!" re-echoed Mr. Cardross, with a start; then recollected himself, and sighed to think how one goes and another comes, and all the world moves on as before— passing, generation after generation, into the awful shadow which no eye except that of faith can penetrate. Life is a little, little day—hardly longer, in the end, for the man in his prime than for the infant of an hour's span.

And the minister, who was of meditative mood, thought to himself much as a poet half a century later put into words — thoughts common to all men, but which only such a man and such a poet could have crystallized into four such perfect lines:

> "Thou wilt not leave us in the dust:
> Thou madest man, he knows not why;
> He thinks he was not made to die,
> And Thou hast made him—Thou art just."

Thus musing, Mr. Cardross followed up stairs toward the magnificent nursery, which had been prepared months before, with a loving eagerness of anticipation, and a merciful blindness to futurity, for the expected heir of the Earls of Cairnforth. For, as before said, the only hope of the lineal continuance of the race was in this one child. It lay in a cradle resplendent with white satin hangings and lace curtains, and beside it sat the nurse — a mere girl, but a widow already—Neil Campbell's widow, whose first child had been born only two days after her husband was drowned. Mr. Cardross knew that she had been sud denly sent for out of the clachan, the countess having, with her dying breath, desired that this young woman, whose circumstances were so like her own, should be taken as wet-nurse to the new-born baby.

.So, in her widow's weeds, grave and sad, but very sweet-looking—she had been a servant at the Castle, and was a rather superior young woman—Janet Campbell took her place beside her charge with an expression in her face as if she felt it was a charge left her by her lost mistress, which must be kept solemnly to the end of her _days—as it was.

The minister shook hands with her silently—she had gone through sore affliction—but the lawyer addressed her in his quick, sharp, business tone, under which he often disguised more emotion than he liked to show.

"You have not been dressing the child? Dr. Hamilton told you not to attempt it."

"Na, na, sir, I didna try," answered Janet, sadly and gently.

"That was well. I'm a father of a family myself," added Mr. Menteith, more gently: "I've six of them; but, thank the Lord, ne'er a one of them like this. Take it on your lap, nurse, and let the minister look at it! Ay, here comes Dr. Hamilton!"

Mr. Cardross knew Dr. Hamilton by repute—as who did not? since at that period it was the widest-known name in the whole medical profession in Scotland. And the first sight of him confirmed the reputation, and made even a stranger recognize that his fame was both natural and justifiable. But the minister had scarcely time to cast a glance on the acute, benevolent, wonderfully powerful and thoughtful head, when his attention was attracted by the poor infant, whom Janet was carefully unswathing from innumerable folds of cotton wool.

Mrs. Campbell was a widow of only a month, and her mistress, to whom she had been much attached, lay dead in the next room, yet she had still a few tears left, and they were dropping like rain over her mistress's child.

No wonder. It lay on her lap, the smallest, saddest specimen of infantile deformity. It had a large head— larger than most infants have—but its body was thin, elf-ish, and distorted, every joint and limb being twisted in some way or other. You could not say that any portion of the child was natural or perfect except the head and face. Whether it had the power of motion or not seem-ed doubtful; at any rate, it made no attempt to move, except feebly turning its head from side to side. It lay, with its large eyes wide open, and at last opened its poor little mouth also, and uttered a loud pathetic wail.

"It greets, doctor, ye hear," said the nurse, eagerly; "'deed, an' it greets fine, whiles."

"A good sign," observed Dr. Hamilton. "Perhaps it may live after all, though one scarcely knows whether to desire it."

"I'll gar it live, doctor," cried Janet, as she rocked and patted it, and at last managed to lay it to her motherly breast; "I'll gar it live, ye'll see! That is, God will-ing."

"It could not live, it could never have lived at all, if He were *not* willing," said the minister, reverently. And then, after a long pause, during which he and the two other gentlemen stood watching, with sad pitying looks, the unfortunate child, he added, so quietly and naturally that, though they might have thought it odd, they could hardly have thought it out of place or hypocritical, "Let us pray."

It was a habit, long familiar to this good Presbyterian minister, who went in and out among his parishioners as their pastor and teacher, consoler and guide. Many a time, in many a cottage, had he knelt down, just as he did here, in the midst of deep affliction, and said a few simple words, as from children to a father—the Father of all men. And the beginning and end of his prayer was, now as always, the expression and experience of his own entire faith—"Thy will be done."

"But what ought *we* to do?" said the Edinburg writer, when, having quitted, not unmoved, the melancholy nursery, he led the way to the scarcely less dreary dining-room, where the two handsome, bright-looking portraits of the late earl and countess still smiled down from the wall—giving Mr. Cardross a start, and making him recall, as if the intervening six weeks had been all a dream, the last day he and Mr. Menteith dined together at that hospitable table. They stole a look at one another, but, with true Scotch reticence, neither exchanged a word. Yet perhaps each respected the other the more, both for the feeling and for its instant repression.

"Whatever we decide to do, ought to be decided now," said Dr. Hamilton, "for I must be in Edinburg to-morrow. And, besides, it is a case in which no medical skill is of much avail, if any: Nature must struggle through—or yield, which I can not help thinking would be the best ending. In Sparta, now, this poor child would have been exposed on Mount—what was the place? to be saved by any opportune death from the still greater misfortune of living."

"But that would have been murder—sheer murder," earnestly replied the minister. "And we are not Spartans, but Christians, to whom the body is not every thing, and who believe that God can work out His wonderful will, if He chooses, through the meanest means—through the saddest tragedies and direst misfortunes. In one sense, Dr. Hamilton, there is no such thing as evil—that is, there is no actual evil in the world except sin."

"There is plenty of that, alas!" said Mr. Menteith. "But as to the child, I wished you to see it—both of you together—if only to bear evidence as to its present condition. For the late earl, in his will, executed, by a most providential chance, the last time I was here, appointed me sole guardian and trustee to a possible widow or child. On me, therefore, depends the charge of this poor infant —the sole bar between those penniless, grasping, altogether discreditable Bruces, and the large property of Cairnforth. You see my position, gentlemen?"

It was not an easy one, and no wonder the honest man looked much troubled.

"I need not say that I never sought it—never thought it possible it would really fall to my lot; but it has fallen, and I must discharge it to the best of my ability. You see what the earl is—born alive, anyhow—though we can hardly wish him to survive."

The three gentlemen were silent. At length Mr. Cardross said,

"There is one worse doubt which has occurred to me.

Do you think, Dr. Hamilton, that the mind is as imperfect as the body? In short, is it not likely that the poor child may turn out to be an idiot?"

"I do not know; and it will be almost impossible to judge for months yet."

"But, idiot or not," cried Mr. Menteith—a regular old Tory, who clung with true conservative veneration to the noble race which he, his father, and grandfather had served faithfully for a century and more—"idiot or not, the boy is undoubtedly Earl of Cairnforth."

"Poor child!"

The gentlemen then sat down and thoroughly discussed the whole matter, finally deciding that, until things appeared somewhat plainer, it was advisable to keep the earl's condition as much as possible from the world in general, and more especially from his own kindred. The Bruces, who lived abroad, would, it was naturally to be concluded—or Mr. Menteith, who had a lawyer's slender faith in human nature, believed so—would pounce down, like eagles upon a wounded lamb, the instant they heard what a slender thread of life hung between them and these great possessions.

Under such circumstances, for the infant to be left unprotected in the solitudes of Loch Beg was very unadvisable; and, besides, it was the guardian's duty to see that every aid which medical skill and surgical science could procure was supplied to a child so afflicted, and upon whose life so much depended. He therefore proposed, and Dr. Hamilton agreed, that immediately after the funeral the little earl should be taken to Edinburg, and placed in the house of the latter, to remain there a year or two, or so long as might be necessary.

Janet Campbell was called in, and expressed herself willing to take her share—no small one—in the responsibility of this plan, if the minister would see to her "ain bairn ;" that was, if the minister really thought the scheme a wise one.

"The minister's opinion seems to carry great weight here," said Dr. Hamilton, smiling.

And it was so; not merely because of his being a minister, but because, with all his gentle, unassuming ways, he had an excellent judgment—the clear, sound, unbiased judgment which no man can ever attain to except a man who thinks little of himself; to whom his own honor and glory come ever second, and his Master's glory and service first. Therefore, both as a man and a minister, Mr. Cardross was equally and wholly reliable: charitable, because he felt his own infirmities; placing himself at no higher level than his neighbor, he was always calmly and scrupulously just. Though a learned, he was not exactly a clever man : probably his sermons, preached every Sunday for the last ten years in Cairnforth Kirk, were neither better nor worse than the generality of country sermons; but that matters little. He was a wise man and a good man, and all his parishioners, scattered over a parish of fourteen Scotch miles, deeply and dearly loved him.

"I think," said Mr. Cardross, "that this plan has many advantages, and is, under the circumstances, the best that could have been ·devised. True, I should like to have had the poor babe under my own eye and my wife's, that we might try to requite in some degree the many kind-nesses we have received from his poor father and mother; but he will be better off in Edinburg. Give him every possible chance of life and health, and a sound mind, and then we must leave the rest to Him, who would not have sent this poor little one into the world at all if He had not had some purpose in so doing, though what that purpose is we can not see. I suppose we shall see it, and many other dark things, some time."

The minister lifted his grave, gentle eyes, and sat looking out upon the familiar view—the sunshiny loch, the green shore, and the far-away circle of mountains—while the other two gentlemen discussed a few other business matters. Then he invited them both to return with him and dine at the Manse, where he and his wife were accustomed to offer to all comers, high and low, rich and poor, "hospitality without grudging."

So the three walked through Cairnforth woods, now glowing with full spring beauty, and wandered about the minister's garden till dinner-time. It was a very simple meal—just the ordinary family dinner, as it was spread day after day, all the year round : they could afford hospitality, but show, with the minister's limited income, was impossible, and he was too honest to attempt it. Many a time the earl himself had dined, merrily and heartily, at that simple table, with the mistress—active, energetic, cheerful, and refined—sitting at the head of it, and the children, a girl and boy, already admitted to take their place there, quiet and well-behaved — brought up from the first to be, like their parents, gentlemen and gentlewomen. The Manse table was a perfect picture of family sunshine and family peace, and, as such, the two Edinburg guests carried away the impression of it in their memories for many a day.

In another week a second stately funeral passed out of the Castle doors, and then they were closed to all comers. By Mr. Menteith's orders, great part of the rooms were shut up, and only two apartments kept for his own use when he came down to look after the estates. It was now fully known that he was the young earl's sole guardian; but so great was the feudal fidelity of the neighborhood, and so entire the respect with which, during an administration of many years, the factor had imbued the Cairnforth tenantry, that not a word was said in objection either to him or to his doings. There was great regret that the poor little earl—the representative of so long and honored a race—was taken away from the admiration of the country-side before even a single soul in the parish, except Mr. and Mrs. Cardross, had set eyes upon him; but still the disappointed gossips submitted, considering that if the minister were satisfied all must be right.

After the departure of Mr. Menteith, Mrs. Campbell, and her charge, a few rumors got abroad that the little earl was "no a' richt"—if an earl could be "no richt"— which the simple folk about Loch Beg and Loch Mhor, accustomed for generations to view the Earls of Cairnforth much as the Thibetians view their Dalai Lama, thought hardly possible. But what was wrong with him nobody precisely knew. The minister did, it was conjectured; but Mr. Cardross was scrupulously silent on the subject; and, with all his gentleness, he was the sort of man to whom nobody ever could address intrusive or impertinent questions.

So, after a while, when the Castle still remained shut

up, curiosity died out, or was only roused at intervals, especially at Mr. Menteith's periodical visits. And to all questions, whether respectfully anxious or merely inquisitive, he never gave but one answer—that the earl was "doing pretty well," and would be back at Cairnforth "some o' these days."

However, that period was so long deferred that the neighbors at last ceased to expect it, or to speculate concerning it. They went about their own affairs, and soon the whole story about the sad death of the late earl and countess, and the birth of the present nobleman, began to be told simply as a story by the elder folk, and slipped out of the younger ones' memories—as, if one only allows it time, every tale, however sad, wicked, or strange, will very soon do. Had it not been for the silent, shut-up castle, standing summer and winter on the loch-side, with its flower-gardens blossoming for none to gather, and its woods—the pride of the whole country—budding and withering, with scarcely a foot to cross, or an eye to notice their wonderful beauty, people would ere long have forgotten the very existence of the last Earl of Cairnforth.

Chapter the Second.

B

It was on a June day—ten years after that bright June day when the minister of Cairnforth had walked with such a sad heart up to Cairnforth Castle, and seen for the first time its unconscious heir — the poor little orphan baby, who in such apparent mockery was called " the Earl." The woods, the hills, the loch, looked exactly the same—nature never changes. As Mr. Cardross walked up to the Castle once more — the first time for many months—in accordance with a request of Mr. Menteith's, who had written to say the earl was coming home, he could hardly believe it was ten years since that sad week when the baby-heir was born, and the countess's funeral had passed out from that now long-closed door.

Mr. Cardross's step was heavier and his face sadder now than then. He who had so often sympathized with others' sorrows had had to suffer patiently his own. From the Manse gate as from that of the Castle, the mother and mistress had been carried, never to return. A new Helen—only fifteen years old—was trying vainly to replace to father and brothers her who was—as Mr. Cardross still touchingly put it—" away." But, though his grief was more than a year old, the minister mourned still. His was one of those quiet natures which make no show, and trouble no one, yet in which sorrow goes deep down, and

grows into the heart, as it were, becoming a part of existence, until existence itself shall cease.

It did not, however, hinder him from doing all his ordinary duties, perhaps with even closer persistence, as he
felt himself sinking into that indifference to outside things
which is the inevitable result of a heavy loss upon any
gentle nature. The fierce rebel against it; the impetu-
ous and impatient throw it off; but the feeble and tender souls make no sign, only quietly pass into that state
which the outer world calls submission and resignation,
yet which is, in truth, mere passiveness—the stolid calm
of a creature that has suffered till it can suffer no more.

The first thing which roused Mr. Cardross out of this
condition, or at least the uneasy recognition that it was
fast approaching, and must be struggled against, consci-
entiously, to the utmost of his power, was Mr. Menteith's
letter, and the request therein concerning Lord Cairnforth.

Without entering much into particulars—it was not
the way of the cautious lawyer—he had stated that, after
ten years' residence in Dr. Hamilton's house, and numer-
ous consultations with every surgeon of repute in Scotland, England—nay, Europe—it had been decided, and
especially at the earnest entreaty of the poor little earl
himself, to leave him to Nature; to take him back to his
native air, and educate him, so far as was possible, in
Cairnforth Castle.

A suitable establishment had accordingly been provided—more servants, and a lady housekeeper or *gouv-
ernante*, who took all external charge of the child, while
the personal care of him was left, as before, to his nurse,

Mrs. Campbell, now wholly devoted to him, for at seven years old her own boy had died. He had another attendant, to whom, with a curious persistency, he had strongly attached himself ever since his babyhood — young Malcolm Campbell, Neil Campbell's brother, who was saved by clinging to the keel of the boat when the late Lord Cairnforth was drowned. Beyond these, whose fond fidelity knew no bounds, there was hardly need of any other person to take charge of the little earl, except a tutor, and that office Mr. Menteith entreated Mr. Cardross to accept.

It was a doubtful point with the minister. He shrank from assuming any new duty, his daily duties being now made only too heavy by the loss of the wife who had shared and lightened them all. But he named the matter to Helen, whom he had lately got into the habit of consulting—she was such a wise little woman for her age —and Helen said anxiously, " Papa, try." Besides, there were six boys to be brought up, and put into the world somehow, and the Manse income was small, and the salary offered by Mr. Menteith very considerable. So when, the second time, Helen's great soft eyes implored silently, " Papa, please try," the minister kissed her, went into his study and wrote to Edinburg his acceptance of the office of tutor to Lord Cairnforth.

What sort of office it would turn out—what kind of instruction he was expected to give, or how much the young earl was capable of receiving, he had not the least idea; but he resolved that, in any case, he would do his duty, and neither man nor minister could be expected to do more.

In pursuance of this resolution, he roused himself that sunny June morning, when he would far rather have sat over his study-fire and let the world go on without him —as he felt it would, easily enough—and walked down to the Castle, where, for the first time these ten years, windows were opened and doors unbarred, and the sweet light and warm air of day let in upon those long-shut rooms, which seemed, in their dumb, inanimate way, glad to be happy again—glad to be made of use once more. Even the portraits of the late earl and countess—he in his Highland dress, and she in her white satin and pearls —both so young and bright, as they looked on the day they were married, seemed to gaze back at each other from either side the long dining-room, as if to say, rejoicingly, "Our son is coming home."

"Have you seen the earl?" said Mr. Cardross to one of the new servants who attended him round the rooms, listening respectfully to all the remarks and suggestions as to furniture and the like which Mr. Menteith had requested him to make. The minister was always special-ly popular with servants and inferiors of every sort, for he possessed, in a remarkable degree, that best key to their hearts, the gentle dignity which never needs to assert a superiority that is at once felt and acknowledged.

"The earl, sir? Na, na"—with a mysterious shake of the head—"naebody sees the earl. Some say—but I hae nae cause to think it mysel'—that he's no a' there."

The minister was sufficiently familiar with that queer, but very expressive Scotch phrase, "not all there," to pursue no farther inquiries. But he sighed, and wished he had delayed a little before undertaking the tutorship.

However, the matter was settled now, and Mr. Cardross was not the man ever to draw back from an agreement or shrink from a promise.

"Whatever the poor child is—even if an idiot," thought he, "I will do my best for him, for his father's and mother's sake."

And he paused several minutes before those bright and smiling portraits, pondering on the mysterious dealings of the great Ruler of the universe—how some are taken and some are left: those removed who seem most happy and most needed; those left behind whom it would have appeared, in our dim and short-sighted judgment, a mercy, both to themselves and others, quietly to have taken away.

But one thing the minister did in consequence of these somewhat sad and painful musings. On his return to the clachan—where, of course, the news of the earl's coming home had long spread, and thrown the whole country-side into a state of the greatest excitement—he gave orders, or at least advice—which was equivalent to orders, since every body obeyed him—that there should be no special rejoicings on the earl's coming home; no bonfire on the hill-side, or triumphal arches across the road, and at the ferry where the young earl would probably land — where, ten years before, the late Earl of Cairnforth had been not landed, but carried, stone-cold, with his hair dripping, and his dead hands still clutching the weeds of the loch. The minister vividly recalled the sight, and shuddered at it still.

"No, no," said he, in talking the matter over with some of his people, whom he went among like a father among his children, true pastor of a most loving flock, "no; we'll wait and see what the earl would like before we make any show. That we are glad to see him he knows well enough, or will very soon find out. And if he should arrive on such a night as this"—looking round on the magnificent June sunset, coloring the mountains at the head of the loch—"he will hardly need a brighter welcome to a bonnier home."

But the earl did not arrive on a gorgeous evening like this, such as come sometimes to the shores of Loch Beg, and make it glow into a perfect paradise: he arrived in "saft" weather—in fact, on a pouring wet Saturday night, and all the clachan saw of him was the outside of his carriage, driving, with closed blinds, down the hill-side. He had taken a long round, and had not crossed the ferry; and he was carried as fast as possible through the dripping wood, reaching, just as darkness fell, the Castle door.

Mr. Cardross, perhaps, should have been there to welcome the child—his conscience rather smote him that he was not—but it was the minister's unbroken habit of years to spend Saturday evening alone in his study. And it might be that, with a certain timidity, inherent in his character, he shrank from this first meeting, and wished to put off as long as possible what must inevitably be awkward, and might be very painful. So, in darkness and rain, unwelcomed save by his own servants, most of whom even had never yet seen him, the poor little earl came to his ancestral door.

But on Sunday morning all things were changed, with one of those sudden changes which make this part of the country so wonderfully beautiful, and so fascinating through its endless variety.

A perfect June day, with the loch glittering in the sun, and the hills beyond it softly outlined with the indistinctness that mountains usually wear in summer, but with the soft summer coloring too, greenish-blue, lilac, and silver-gray varying continually. In the woods behind, where the leaves were already gloriously green, the wood-pigeons were cooing, and the blackbirds and mavises singing, just as if it had not been Sunday morning, or rather as if they knew it was Sunday, and were straining their tiny throats to bless the Giver of sweet, peaceful, cheerful Sabbath-days, and of all other good things, meant for man's usage and delight.

At the portico of Cairnforth Castle, for the first time since the hearse had stood there, stood a carriage—one of those large, roomy, splendid family carriages which were in use many years ago. Looking at it, no passer-by could have the slightest doubt that it was my lord's coach, and that my lord sat therein in solemn state, exacting and receiving an amount of respect little short of veneration, such as, for generations, the whole country-side had always paid to the Earls of Cairnforth. This coach, though it was the identical family coach, had been newly furnished; its crimson satin glowed, and its silver harness and ornaments flashed in the sun; the coachman sat in his place, and two footmen stood up in their places behind. It was altogether a very splendid affair, as became the equipage of a young nobleman who was known to possess twenty thousand a year, and who, from his castle tower—it had a tower, though nobody ever climbed

B 2

there—might, if he chose, look around upon miles and
miles of moorland, loch, hill-side, and cultivated land, and
say to himself—or be said to by his nurse, as in the old
song—

> "These hills and these vales, from this tower that ye see,
> They all shall belong, my young chieftain, to thee."

The horses pawed the ground for several minutes of
delay, and then there appeared Mr. Menteith, followed by
Mrs. Campbell, who was quite a grand lady now, in silks
and satins, but with the same sweet, sad, gentle face. The
lawyer and she stood aside, and made way for a big, stalwart young Highlander of about one-and-twenty or there-
abouts, who carried in his arms, very gently and carefully, wrapped in a plaid, even although it was such a mild
spring day, what looked like a baby, or a very young
child.

"Stop a minute, Malcolm."

At the sound of that voice, which was not an infant's,
though it was thin, and sharp, and unnatural rather for
a boy, the big Highlander paused immediately.

"Hold me up higher; I want to look at the loch."

"Yes, my lord."

This, then—this poor little deformed figure, with every
limb shrunken and useless, and every joint distorted, the
head just able to sustain itself and turn feebly from one
side to the other, and the thin white hands piteously
twisted and helpless-looking—this, then, was the Earl of
Cairnforth.

"It's a bonnie loch, Malcolm."

"It looks awfu' bonnie the day, my lord."

"And," almost in a whisper, "was it just there my father was drowned?"

"Yes, my lord."

No one spoke while the large, intelligent eyes, which seemed the principal feature of the thin face, that rested against Malcolm's shoulder, looked out intently upon the loch.

Mrs. Campbell pulled her veil down and wept a little. People said Neil Campbell had not been the best of husbands to her; but he was her husband; and she had never been back in Cairnforth till now, for her son had lived, died, and been buried away in Edinburg.

At last Mr. Menteith suggested that the kirk bell was beginning to ring.

"Very well; put me into the carriage."

Malcolm placed him, helpless as an infant, in a corner of the silken-padded coach, fitted with cushions especially suited for his comfort. There he sat, in his black velvet coat and point-lace collar, with silk stockings and dainty shoes upon the poor little feet that never had walked, and never would walk, in this world. The one bit of him that could be looked at without pain was his face, inherited from his beautiful mother. It was wan, pale, and much older than his years, but it was a sweet face—a lovely face; so patient, thoughtful—nay, strange to say, content. You could not look at it without a certain sense of peace, as if God, in taking away so much, had given something—which not many people have—something which was the divine answer to the minister's prayer over the two-days-old child—"Thy will be done."

"Are you comfortable, my lord?"

"Quite, thank you, Mr. Menteith. Stop — where are you going, Malcolm?"

"Just to the kirk, and I'll be there as soon as your lordship."

"Very well," said the little earl, and watched with wistful eyes the tall Highlander striding across brushwood and heather, leaping dikes and clearing fences— the very embodiment of active, vigorous youth.

Wistful I said the eyes were, and yet they were not sad. Whatever thoughts lay hidden in that boy's mind —he was only ten years old, remember—they were certainly not thoughts of melancholy or despair. "God tempers the wind to the shorn lamb," and "the back is fitted to the burden," are phrases so common that we almost smile to repeat them or believe in them, and yet they are true. Any one whose enjoyments have been narrowed down by long sickness may prove their truth by recollecting how at last even the desire for impossible pleasures passes away. And in this case the deprivation was not sudden; the child had been born thus crippled, and had never been accustomed to any other sort of existence than this. What thoughts, speculations, or regrets might have passed through his mind, or whether he had as yet reflected upon his own condition at all, those about him could not judge. He was always a silent child, and latterly had grown more silent than ever. It was this silence, causing a fear lest the too rapidly developing mind might affect still more injuriously the imperfect and feeble body, which induced his guardian, counseled by Dr. Hamilton, to try a total change of life by sending him home to the shores of Loch Beg.

One thing certainly Mr. Cardross need not have dreaded—the child was no idiot. An intelligence, precocious to an almost painful extent, was visible in that poor little face, which seemed thirstingly to take in every thing, and to let nothing escape its observation.

The carriage drove slowly through the woods and along the shore of the loch, Mr. Menteith and Mrs. Campbell sitting opposite to the earl, not noticing him much—even as a child he was sensitive of being watched—but making occasional comments on the scenery and other things.

"There is the kirk tower; I mind it weel," said Mrs. Campbell, who still kept some accent of the clachan, though, like many Highlanders, she had it more in tone than in pronunciation, and often spoke almost pure English, which, indeed, she had taken pains to acquire, lest she might be transferred from her charge for fear of teaching him to speak as a young nobleman ought not to speak. But at sight of her native place some touch of the old tongue returned.

"That is the kirk, nurse, where my father and mother are buried?"

"Yes, my lord."

"Will there be many people there? You know I never went to church but once before in all my life."

"Would ye like not to go now? If so, I'll turn back with ye this minute, my lamb—my lord, I mean."

"No, thank you, nurse, I like to go. You know Mr. Menteith promised me I should go about every where as soon as I came to live at Cairnforth."

"Every where you like that is not too much trouble

to your lordship," said Mr. Menteith, who was always tenaciously careful about the respect, of word and act, that he paid, and insisted should be paid, to his poor young ward.

"Oh, it's no trouble to me; Malcolm takes care of that. And I like to see the world. If you and Dr. Hamilton would have let me, I think I would so have enjoyed going to school like other boys."

"Would you, my lord?" answered Mr. Menteith, compassionately; but Mrs. Campbell, who never could bear that pitying look and tone directed toward her nursling, said, a little sharply,

"It's better as it is—dinna ye ken? Far mair fitting for his lordship's rank and position that he should get his learning all by himsel' at his ain castle, and with his ain tutor, and that sic a gentleman as Mr. Cardross—"

"What is Mr. Cardross like?"

"Ye'll hear him preach the day."

"Will he teach me all by myself, as nurse says? Has he any children—any boys, like me?"

"He has boys," said Mr. Menteith, avoiding more explicit information; for with a natural, if mistaken precaution, he had always kept his own sturdy, stalwart boys quite out of the way of the poor little earl, and had especially cautioned the minister to do the same.

"I do long to play with boys. May I?"

"If you wish it, my lord."

"And may I have a boat on that beautiful loch, and be rowed about just where I please? Malcolm says it would not shake me nearly so much as the carriage. May I go to the kirk every Sunday, and see every thing and every body, and read as many books as ever I choose? Oh, how happy I shall be! — as happy as a king!"

"God help thee, my lamb!" muttered Mrs. Campbell to herself, while even Mr. Menteith turned his face sedu- lously toward the loch and took snuff violently.

By this time they had reached the church door, where the congregation were already gathering and hanging about, as Scotch congregations do, till service begins. But of this service and this Sunday, which was so strangely momentous a day in more lives than one, the next chap- ter must tell.

Chapter the Third.

THE carriage of the Earl of Cairnforth, with its familiar and yet long unfamiliar liveries, produced a keen sensation among the simple folk who formed the congregation of Cairnforth. But they had too much habitual respect for the great house and great folk of the place, mingled with their national shyness and independence, to stare very much. A few moved aside to make way for the two grand Edinburg footmen who leaped down from their perch in order to render customary assistance to the occupants of the carriage.

Mrs. Campbell and Mr. Menteith descended first, and then the two footmen looked puzzled as to what they should do next.

But Malcolm was before them—Malcolm, who never suffered mortal man but himself to render the least assistance to his young master; who watched and tended him; waited on and fed him in the day, and slept in his room at night; who, in truth, had now, for a year past, slipped into all the offices of a nurse as well as servant, and performed them with a woman's tenderness, care, and skill. Lord Cairnforth's eyes brightened when he saw him; and, carried in Malcolm's arms—a few stragglers of the congregation standing aside to let them pass —the young earl was brought to the door of the kirk where his family had worshiped for generations.

Two elders stood there beside the plate—white-headed farmers, who remembered both the late lord and the one before him.

"Yon's the earl," whispered they, and came forward respectfully; then, startled by the unexpected and piti-ful sight, they shrank back; but either the boy did not notice this, or was so used to it that he showed no sur-prise.

"My purse, Malcolm," the small, soft voice was heard to say.

"Ay, my lord. What will ye put into the plate?"

"A guinea, I think, to - day, because I am so very happy."

This answer, which the two elders overheard, was told by them next day to every body, and remembered along the loch-side for years.

Cairnforth Kirk, like most other Scotch churches of ancient date, is very plain within and without, and the congregation then consisted almost entirely of hill-side farmers, shepherds, and the like, who arrived in families —dogs and all, for the dogs always came to church, and behaved there as decorously as their masters. Many of the people walked eight, ten, and even twelve miles, from the extreme boundary of the parish, and waited about in the kirk or kirk-yard on fine Sundays, and in the Manse kitchen on wet ones—which were much the most fre-quent—during the two hours' interval between sermons.

In the whole congregation there was hardly a person above the laboring class except in the minister's pew and that belonging to the Castle, which had been newly lined and cushioned, and in a corner of which, safely deposited

by Malcolm, the little earl now sat—sat always, even
during the prayer, at which some of the congregation
looked reprovingly round, but only saw the little figure
wrapped in a plaid, and the sweet, wan, childish, and yet
unchild-like face, with the curly dark hair, and large
dark eyes.

Whatever in the earl was "no a' richt," it certainly
could not be his mind, for a brighter, more intelligent
countenance was never seen. It quite startled the minister with the intentness of its gaze from the moment he
ascended the pulpit; and though he tried not to look
that way, and was very nervous, he could not get over
the impression it made. It was to him almost like a face
from the grave—this strange, eerie child's face, so strongly resembling that of the dead countess, who, despite the
difference in rank, had, during the brief year she lived
and reigned at Cairnforth, been almost like an equal
friend and companion to his own dead wife. Their two
faces—Lady Cairnforth's as she looked the last time he
saw her in her coffin, and his wife's as she lay in hers—
mingled together, and affected him powerfully.

The good minister was not remarkable for the brillian-
cy of his sermons, which he wrote and "committed"—that
is, learned by heart, to deliver in pseudo-extempore fashion, as was the weary custom of most Scotch ministers
of his time. But this Sunday, all that he had committed
slipped clean out of his memory. He preached as he had
never been known to preach before, and never preached again—with originality, power, eloquence; speaking
from his deepest heart, as if the words thence pouring out
had been supernaturally put into it; which, with a su-

perstition that approached to sublimest faith, he afterward solemnly believed they had been.

The text was that verse about "all things working together for good to them that love God;" but, whatever the original discourse had been, it wandered off into a subject which all who knew the minister recognized as one perpetually close to his heart—submission to the will of God, whatever that will might be, and however incomprehensible it seemed to mortal eyes.

"Not, my friends," said he, after speaking for a long time on this head—speaking rather than sermonizing, which, like many cultivated but not very original minds, he was too prone to do—"not that I would encourage or excuse that weak yielding to calamity which looks like submission, but is, in fact, only cowardice; submitting to all things as to a sort of fatality, without struggling against them, or trying to distinguish how much of them is the will of God, and how much our own weak will; daunted by the first shadow of misfortune, especially misfortunes in our worldly affairs, wherein so much often happens for which we have ourselves only to blame. Submission to man is one thing, submission to God another. The latter is divine, the former is often merely contemptible. But even to the Almighty Father we should yield not a blind, crushed resignation, but an open-eyed obedience, like that we would fain win from our own children, desiring to make of them children, not slaves.

"My children—for I speak to the very youngest of you here, and do try to understand me if you can, or as much as you can—it is right—it is God's will—that you should resist, to the very last, any trial which is not in-evitable. There are in this world countless sorrows, which, so far as appears, we actually bring on ourselves and others by our own folly, wickedness, or weakness— which is often as fatal as wickedness; and then we blame Providence for it, and sink into total despair. But when, as sometimes happens, His heavy hand is laid upon us in a visible, inevitable misfortune which we can not strug-gle against, and from which no human aid can save us, then we ought to learn His hardest lesson—to submit. To submit—yet still, while saying 'Thy will be done,' to strive, so far as we can, *to do it.* If He have taken from us all but one talent, even that, my children, let us not bury in a napkin. Let us rather put it out at usury, leaving to Him to determine how much we shall receive again; for it is according to our use of what we have, and not of what we have not, that He will call us 'good and faithful servants,' and at last, when the long struggle of living shall be over, will bid us 'enter into the joy of our Lord.' "

When the minister sat down, he saw, as he had seen, consciously or unconsciously, all through the service, and above the entire congregation, those two large intent eyes fixed upon him from the Cairnforth pew.

Children of ten years old do not usually listen much to sermons, but the little earl had heard very few, for it was difficult to take him to church without so many peo-ple staring at him. Nevertheless, he listened to this ser-mon, so plain and clear, suited to the capacity of ignorant shepherds and little children, and seemed as if he under-stood it all. If he did not then, he did afterward.

When service was over, he sat watching the congregation pass out, especially noticing a family of boys who
occupied the adjoining pew. They had neither father
nor mother with them, but an elder sister, as she appeared to be—a tall girl of about fifteen. She marshaled
them out before her, not allowing them once to turn, as
many of the other people did, to look with curiosity at
the poor little earl. But in quitting the kirk she stopped
at the vestry door, apparently to say a word to the minister; after which Mr. Cardross came forward, his gown
over his arm, and spoke to Mr. Menteith—

"Where is Lord Cairnforth? I was so glad to see him
here."

"Thank you, Mr. Cardross," replied a weak but cheerful voice from Malcolm's shoulder, which so startled the
good minister that he found not another word for a whole
minute. At last he said, hesitating,

"Helen has just been reminding me that the earl and
countess used always to come and rest at the Manse between sermons. Would Lord Cairnforth like to do the
same? It is a good way to the Castle—or perhaps he is
too fatigued for the afternoon service?"

"Oh no, I should like it very much. And, nurse, I do
so want to see Mr. Cardross's children; and Helen—who
is Helen?"

"My daughter. Come here, Helen, and speak to the
earl."

She came forward—the tall girl who had sat at the end
of the pew, in charge of the six boys—came forward in
her serious, gentle, motherly way—alas! she was the only
mother at the Manse now—and put out her hand, but in-

stinctively drew it back again; for oh! what poor, helpless, unnatural-looking fingers were feebly advanced an
inch or so to meet hers! They actually shocked her—
gave her a sick sense of physical repulsion; but she conquered it. Then, by a sudden impulse of conscience,
quite forgetting the rank of the earl, and only thinking
of the poor, crippled, orphaned baby—for he seemed no
more than a baby—Helen did what her warm, loving
heart was in the habit of doing, as silent consolation for
every thing, to her own tribe of "mitherless bairns"—
she stooped forward and kissed him.

The little earl was so astonished that he blushed up to
the very brow. But from that minute he loved Helen
Cardross, and never ceased loving her to the end of his
days.

She led the way to the Manse, which was so close behind the kirk that the back windows of it looked on the
grave-yard. But in front there was a beautiful lawn and
garden—the prettiest Manse garden that ever was seen.
Helen stepped through it with her light, quick step, a
child clinging to each hand, often turning round to speak
to Malcolm or to the earl. He followed her with his eyes,
and thought she was like a picture he had once seen of a
guardian angel leading two children along, though there
was not a bit of the angel about Helen Cardross—externally at least, she being one of those large, rosy, round-
faced, flaxen-haired Scotch girls who are far from pretty
even in youth, and in middle age sometimes grow quite
coarse and plain. She would not do so, and did not; for
any body so good, so sweet, so bright, must always carry
about with her, even to old age, something which, if not

C

beauty's self, is beauty's atmosphere, and which often cre-
ates, even around unlovely people, a light and glory as
perfect as the atmosphere round the sun.

She took her seat—her poor mother's that used to be
—at the head of the Manse table—which was a little qui-
eter on Sundays than week-days, and especially this Sunday, when the children were all awed and shy before
their new visitor. Helen had previously taken them all
aside, and explained to them that they were not to notice
any thing in the earl that was different from other people—that he was a poor little crippled boy who had neither father, mother, brother, nor sister; that they were
to be very kind to him, but not to look at him much, and
to make no remarks upon him on any account whatever.

And so, even though he was placed on baby's high
chair, and fed by Malcolm almost as if he were a baby—
he who, though no bigger than a baby, was in reality a
boy of ten years old, whom papa talked to, and who talked
with papa almost as cleverly as Helen herself—still the
Manse children were so well behaved that nothing occurred to make any body uncomfortable.

For the little earl, he seemed to enjoy himself amazingly. He sat in his high chair, and looked round the well-
filled table with mingled curiosity and amusement; inquired the children's names, and was greatly interested
in the dog, the cat, a rabbit, and two kittens, which after
dinner they successively brought to amuse him. And
then he invited them all to the Castle next day, and promised to take them over his garden there.

"But how can you take us?" said the youngest, in
spite of Helen's frown. "We can run about, but you—"

"I can't run about, that is true; but I have a little carriage, and Malcolm draws it, or Malcolm carries me, and
then I can see such a deal. I used to see nothing—only
lie on a sofa all day, and have doctors coming about me
and hurting me," added the poor little earl, growing confidential, as one by one the boys slipped away, leaving
him alone with Helen.

"Did they hurt you very much?" asked she.

"Oh, terribly; but I never told. You see, there was
no use in telling; it could not be helped, and it would
only have made nurse cry—she always cries over me. I
think that is why I like Malcolm; he always helps me,
and he never cries. And I am getting a great boy now;
I was ten years old last week."

Ten years old, though he seemed scarcely more than
five, except by the old look of his face. But Helen took
no notice, only saying "that she hoped the doctors did
not hurt him now."

"No, that is all over. Dr. Hamilton says I am to be
left to Nature, whatever that is; I overheard him say it
one day. And I begged of Mr. Menteith not to shut me
up any longer, or take me out only in my carriage, but
to let me go about as I like, Malcolm carrying me—isn't
he a big, strong fellow? You can't think how nice it is
to be carried about, and see every thing—oh, it makes
me so happy!"

The tone in which he said "so happy" made the tears
start to Helen's eyes. She turned away to the window,
where she saw her own big brothers, homely - featured
and coarsely clad, but full of health, and strength, and activity, and then looked at this poor boy, who had every

thing that fortune could give, and yet—nothing! She thought how they grumbled and squabbled, those rough lads of hers; how she herself often felt the burden of the large narrow household more than she could bear, and lost heart and temper; then she thought of him—poor, helpless soul!—you could hardly say body—who could neither move hand nor foot—who was dependent as an infant on the kindness or compassion of those about him. Yet he talked of being "so happy!" And there entered into Helen Cardross's good heart toward the Earl of Cairnforth a deep tenderness, which from that hour nothing ever altered or estranged.

It was not pity—something far deeper. Had he been fretful, fractious, disagreeable, she would still have been very sorry for him and very kind to him. But now, to see him as he was—cheerful, patient; so ready with his interest in others, so utterly without envyings and complainings regarding himself—changed what would otherwise have been mere compassion into actual reverence. As she sat beside him in his little chair, not looking at him much, for she still found it difficult to overcome the painful impression of the sight of that crippled and deformed body, she felt a choking in her throat and a dimness in her eyes—a longing to do any thing in the wide world that would help or comfort the poor little earl.

"Do you learn any lessons?" asked she, thinking he seemed to enjoy talking with her. "I thought at dinner to-day that you seemed to know a great many things."

"Did I? That is very odd, for I fancied I knew nothing; and I want to learn every thing—if Mr. Cardross will teach me. I should like to sit and read all day long.

I could do it by myself, now that I have found out a way
of holding the book and turning over the leaves without
nurse's helping me. Malcolm invented it—Malcolm is
so clever and so kind."

"Is Malcolm always with you?"

"Oh yes; how could I do without Malcolm? And
you are quite sure your father will teach me every thing
I want to learn?" pursued the little earl, very eagerly.

Helen was quite sure.

"And there is another thing. Mr. Menteith says I must
try, if possible, to learn to write—if only so as to be able
to sign my name. In eleven more years, when I am a
man, he says I shall often be required to sign my name.
Do you think I could manage to learn?"

Helen looked at the poor, twisted, powerless fingers,
and doubted it very much. Still she said cheerfully, "It
would anyhow be a good thing to try."

"So it would—and I'll try. I'll begin to-morrow.
Will you"—with a pathetic entreaty in the soft eyes—
"it might be too much trouble for Mr. Cardross—but will
you teach me?"

"Yes, my dear!" said Helen, warmly, "that I will."

"Thank you. And"—still hesitating—"please would
you always call me 'my dear' instead of 'my lord;' and
might I call you Helen?"

So they "made a paction 'twixt them twa"—the poor
little helpless, crippled boy, and the bright, active, energetic girl—the earl's son and the minister's daughter—
one of those pactions which grow out of an inner simili-
tude which counteracts all outward dissimilarity; and
they never broke it while they lived.

"Has my lamb enjoyed himself?" inquired Mrs. Campbell, anxiously and affectionately, when she reappeared from the Manse kitchen. Then, with a sudden resumption of dignity, "I beg your pardon, Miss Cardross, but this is the first time his lordship has ever been out to dinner."

"Oh, nurse, how I wish I might go out to dinner every Sunday! I am sure this has been the happiest day of all my life."

Chapter the Fourth.

IF the "happiest day in all his life" had been the first day the earl spent at Cairnforth Manse, which very likely it was, he took the first possible opportunity of renewing his happiness.

Early on Monday forenoon, while Helen's ever-active hands were still busy clearing away the six empty porridge plates, and the one tea-cup which had contained the beverage which the minister loved, but which was too dear a luxury for any but the father of the family, Malcolm Campbell's large shadow was seen darkening the window.

"There's the earl!" cried Helen, whose quick eye had already caught sight of the white little face muffled up in Malcolm's plaid, and the soft black curls resting on his shoulder, damp with rain, and blown about by the wind, for it was what they called at Loch Beg a "coarse" day.

"My lord was awfu' set upon coming," said Malcolm, apologetically; "and when my lord taks a thing into his heid, he'll aye do't, ye ken."

"We are very glad to see the earl," returned the minister, who nevertheless looked a little perplexed; for, while finishing his breakfast, he had been confiding to Helen how very nervous he felt about this morning's

C 2

duties at the Castle—how painful it would be to teach a child so afflicted, and how he wished he had thought twice before he undertook the charge. And Helen had been trying to encourage him by telling him all that had passed between herself and the boy—how intelligent he had seemed, and how eager to learn. Still, the very fact that they had been discussing him made Mr. Cardross feel slightly confused. Men shrink so much more than women from any physical suffering or deformity; besides, except those few moments in the church, this was really the first time he had beheld Lord Cairnforth; for on Sundays it was the minister's habit to pass the whole time between sermons in his study, and not join the family table until tea.

"We are very glad to see the earl at all times," repeated he, but hesitatingly, as if not sure that he was quite speaking the truth.

"Yes, very glad," added Helen, hastily, fancying she could detect in the prematurely acute and sensitive face a consciousness that he was not altogether welcome. "My father was this minute preparing to start for the Castle."

"My lord didna like to trouble the minister to be walking out this coarse day," said Malcolm, with true Highland ingenuity of politeness. "His lordship thocht that instead o' Mr. Cardross coming to him, he would just come to Mr. Cardross."

"No, Malcolm," interposed the little voice, "it was not exactly that. I wished for my own sake to come to the Manse again, and to ask if I might come every day and take my lessons here—it's so dreary in that big library.

I'll not be much trouble, indeed, sir," he added, entreat-
ingly; "Malcolm will carry me in and carry me out. I
can sit on almost any sort of chair now; and with this
wee bit of stick in my hand I can turn over the leaves
of my books my very own self—I assure you I can."

The minister walked to the window. He literally
could not speak for a minute, he felt so deeply moved,
and in his secret heart so very much ashamed of himself.

When he turned round Malcolm had placed the little
figure in an arm-chair by the fire, and was busy unswathing the voluminous folds of the plaid in which it had
been wrapped. Helen, after a glance or two, pretended
to be equally busy over her daily duty—the common
duty of Scotch housewives at that period—of washing
up the delicate china with her own neat hands, and putting it safe away in the parlor press; for, as before said,
Mr. Cardross's income was very small, and, like that of
most country ministers, very uncertain, his stipend alter-
ing year by year, according to the price of corn. They
kept one "lassie" to help, but Helen herself had to do a
great deal of the housework. She went on doing it now,
as probably she would in any case, being at once too simple and too proud to be ashamed of it; still, she was glad
to seem busy, lest the earl might have fancied she was
watching him.

Her feminine instinct had been right. Now for the
first time taken out of his shut-up nursery life, where he
himself had been the principal object—where he had no
playfellows and no companions save those he had been
used to from infancy—removed from this, and brought
into ordinary family life, the poor child felt—he could

not but feel—the sad, sad difference between himself and all the rest of the world. His color came and went—he looked anxiously, deprecatingly, at Mr. Cardross.

"I hope, sir, you are not displeased with me for coming to-day. I shall not be very much trouble to you—at least I will try to be as little trouble as I can."

"My boy," said the minister, crossing over to him and laying his hand upon his head, "you will not be the least trouble; and if you were ever so much, I would cheerfully undertake it for the sake of your father and mother, and—" he added, more to himself than aloud—"for your own."

That was true. Nature, which is never without her compensations, had put into this child of ten years old a strange charm, an inexpressible loveableness—that loveableness which springs from lovingness, though every loving nature is not fortunate enough to possess it. But the earl's did; and as he looked up into the minister's face, with that touchingly grateful expression he had, the good man felt his heart melt and brim over at his eyes.

"You don't dislike me, then, because—because I am not like other boys?"

Mr. Cardross smiled, though his eyes were still dim, and his voice not clear; and with that smile vanished forever the slight repulsion he had felt to the poor child. He took him permanently into his good heart, and from his manner the earl at once knew that it was so.

He brightened up immediately.

"Now, Malcolm, carry me in; I'm quite ready," said he, in a tone which indicated that quality, discernible

even at so early an age—a "will of his own." To see
the way he ordered Malcolm about—the big fellow obey-
ing him, with something beyond even the large limits of
that feudal respect which his forbears had paid to the
earl's forbears for many a generation, was a sight at once
touching and hopeful.

"There—put me into the child's chair I had at dinner
yesterday. Now fetch me a pillow—or rather roll up
your plaid into one—don't trouble Miss Cardross. That
will make me quite comfortable. Pull out my books
from your pouch, Malcolm, and spread them out on the
table, and then go and have a crack with your old friends
at the clachan; you can come for me in two hours."

It was strange to see the little figure giving its orders,
and settling itself with the preciseness of an old man at
the study-table; but still this removed somewhat of the
painful shyness and uncomfortableness from every body,
and especially from Mr. Cardross. He sat himself down
in his familiar arm-chair, and looked across the table at
his poor little pupil, who seemed at once so helpless and
so strong.

Lessons begun. The child was exceedingly intelligent
—precociously, nay, preternaturally so, it appeared to Mr.
Cardross, who, like many another learned father, had been
blessed with rather stupid boys, who liked any thing better than study, and whom he had with great labor dragged through a course of ordinary English, Latin, and
even a fragment of Greek. But this boy seemed all
brains. His cheeks flushed, his eyes glittered, he learned
as if he actually enjoyed learning. True, as Mr. Cardross
soon discovered, his acquirements were not at all in the

regular routine of education; he was greatly at fault in
many simple things; but the amount of heterogeneous
and out-of-the-way knowledge which he had gathered up,
from all available sources, was quite marvelous. And,
above all, to teach a boy unto whom learning seemed a
pleasure rather than a torment, a favor instead of a pun-
ishment, was such an exceeding and novel delight to the
good minister, that soon he forgot the crippled figure—
the helpless hands that sometimes with fingers, sometimes
even with teeth, painfully guided the ingeniously cut
forked stick, and the thin face that only too often turned
white and weary, but quickly looked up, as if struggling
against weakness, and concentrating all attention on the
work that was to be done.

At twelve o'clock Helen came in with her father's
lunch—a foaming glass of new milk, warm from the cow.
The little earl looked at it with eager eyes.

"Will I bring you one too?" said Helen.

"Oh—thank you; I am so thirsty. And, please, would
you move me a little—just a very little; I don't often
sit so long in one position. It won't trouble you very
much, will it?"

"Not at all, if you will only show me how," stam-
mered Helen, turning hot and red. But, shaking off her
hesitation, she lifted up the poor child tenderly and carefully, shook his pillows and "sorted" him according to
her own untranslatable Scotch word, then went quickly
out of the room to compose herself, for she had done it
all, trembling exceedingly the while. And yet, somehow, a feeling of great tenderness—tenderer than even
she had felt successively toward her own baby brothers,

had grown up in her heart toward him, taking away every possible feeling of repulsion on account of his deformity.

She brought back the glass of creamy milk and a bit of oatcake, and laid them beside the earl. He regarded them wistfully.

"How nice the milk looks! I am so tired — and so thirsty. Please—would you give me some? Just hold the glass, that's all, and I can manage."

Helen held it to his lips—the first time she ever did so, but not the last by many. Years and years from then, when she herself was quite an old woman, she remembered giving him that drink of milk, and how, afterward, two large soft eyes were turned upon hers so lovingly, so gratefully, as if the poor cripple had drank in something besides milk—the sweet draught of human affection, not dried up even to such heavily afflicted ones as he.

"Are lessons all done for to-day, papa?" said she, noticing that, eager as it was, the little face looked very wan and wearied, but also noticing with delight that her father's expression was brighter and more interested than it had been this long time.

"Done, Helen? Well, if my pupil is tired, certainly."

"But I'm not tired, sir."

Helen shook her motherly head: "Quite enough for to-day. You may come back again to-morrow."

He did come back. Day after day, in fair weather or foul, big Malcolm was to be seen stepping with his free Highland step—Malcolm was a lissome, handsome young fellow—across the Manse garden, carrying that small, frail burden, which all the inhabitants of the clachan had ceased to stare at, and to which they all raised their bonnets or touched their shaggy forelocks. "It's the wee earl, ye ken," and one and all treated with the utmost respect the tiny figure wrapped in a plaid, so that nothing was visible except a small child's face, which always smiled at sight of other children.

It was surprising in how few days the clachan, and indeed the whole neighborhood, grew accustomed to the appearance of the earl and his sad story. Perhaps this was partly due to Helen and Mr. Cardross, who, seeing no longer any occasion for mystery, indeed regretting a little that any mystery had ever been made about the matter, took every opportunity of telling every body who inquired the whole facts of the case.

These were few enough and simple enough, though very sad. The Earl—the last Earl of Cairnforth—was a hopeless cripple for life. All the consultations of all the doctors had resulted in that conclusion. It was very unlikely he would ever be better than he was now physically, but mentally he was certainly "a' richt"—or "a' there," as the country-folk express it. There was, as Mr. Cardross carefully explained to every body, not the slightest ground for supposing him deficient in intellect; on the contrary, his intellect seemed almost painfully acute. The quickness with which he learned his lessons surpassed that of any boy of his age the minister had ever known; and he noticed every thing around him so closely, and made such intelligent remarks, that to talk with him was like talking with a grown man. Before the first week was over Mr. Cardross began actually to enjoy the child's company, and to look forward to lesson hours as the pleasantest hours of his day; for, since the Castle was closed, the minister's lot had been the almost inevitable lot of a country clergyman, whose parish con tains many excellent people, who look up to him with the utmost reverence, and for whom he entertains the sincere respect that worth must always feel toward worth, but with whom he had very few intellectual sympathies. In truth, since Mrs. Cardross died the minister had shut himself up almost entirely, and had scarcely had a single interest out of his own study until the earl came home to Cairnforth.

Now, after lessons, he would occasionally be persuaded to quit that beloved study, and take a walk along the loch side, or across the moor, to show his pupil the coun· try of which he, poor little fellow! was owner and lord. He did it at first out of pure kindness, to save the earl from the well·meant intrusion of neighbors, but afterward from sheer pleasure in seeing the boy so happy. To him, mounted in Malcolm's arms, and brought for the first time into contact with the outer world, every thing was a novelty and delight. And his quick perception let nothing escape him. He seemed to watch lovingly all nature, from the grand lights and shadows which moved over the mountains, to the little moorland flowers which he made Malcolm stop to gather. All living things too, from the young rabbit that scudded across their path, to the lark that rose singing up into the wide blue air—he saw and noticed every thing.

But he never once said, what Helen, who, as often as

her house duties allowed, delighted to accompany them
on these expeditions, was always expecting he would
say, Why had God given these soulless creatures legs to
run and wings to fly, strength, health, and activity to enjoy existence, and denied all these things to him? Denied them, not for a week, a month, a year, but for his
whole lifetime—a lifetime so short at best;—"few of
days, and full of trouble." Why could He not have
made it a little more happy?

Thousands have asked themselves, in some form or
other, the same unanswered, unanswerable question. Hel-
en had done so already, young as she was; when her
mother died, and her father seemed slowly breaking
down, and the whole world appeared to her full of darkness and woe. How then must it have appeared to this
poor boy? But, strange to say, that bitter doubt, which
so often came into Helen's heart, never fell from the
child's lips at all. Either he was still a mere child, accepting life just as he saw it, and seeking no solution of
its mysteries, or else, though so young, he was still strong
enough to keep his doubts to himself, to bear his own
burden, and trouble no one.

Or else — and when she watched his inexpressibly
sweet face, which had the look you sometimes see in
blind faces, of absolutely untroubled peace, Helen was
forced to believe this—God, who had taken away from
him so much, had given him something still more—a
spiritual insight so deep and clear that he was happy in
spite of his heavy misfortune. She never looked at him
but she thought involuntarily of the text, out of the only
book with which unlearned Helen was very familiar—

that "in heaven their angels do always behold the face of my Father which is in heaven."

After a fortnight's stay at the Castle Mr. Menteith felt convinced that his experiment had succeeded, and that, onerous as the duty of guardian was, he might be satisfied to leave his ward under the charge of Mr. Cardross.

"Only, if those Bruces should try to get at him, you must let me know at once. Remember, I trust you."

"Certainly you may. Has any thing been heard of them lately?"

"Nothing much, beyond the continual applications for advances of the annual sum which the late earl gave them, and which I continue to pay, just to keep them out of the way."

"They are still abroad?"

"I suppose so; but I hear very little about them. They were relations on the countess's side, you know—it was she who brought the money. Poor little fellow, what an accumulation it will be by the time he is of age, and what small good it will do him!"

And the honest man sighed as he looked from Mr. Cardross's dining-room window across the Manse garden, where, under a shady tree, was placed the earl's little wheel-chair, which was an occasional substitute for Malcolm's arms. In it he sat, with a book on his lap, and with that aspect of entire content which was so very touching. Helen sat beside him on the grass, sewing—she was always sewing; and, indeed, she had need, if her needle were to keep pace with its requirements in that large family of boys.

"That's a good girl of yours, and his lordship seems to

have taken to her amazingly. I am very glad, for he
had no feminine company at all except Mrs. Campbell,
and, good as she is, she isn't quite the thing—not exactly
a lady, you see. Eh, Mr. Cardross — what a lady his
mother was! We'll never again see the like of the poor
countess, nor, in all human probability, will we ever again
see another Countess of Cairnforth."

"No."

"Yet," continued Mr. Menteith, after a long pause,
"Dr. Hamilton thinks he may live many years. Strange
to say, his constitution is healthy and sound, and his
sweet, placid nature — his mother's own nature (isn't he
very like her sometimes?) — gives him so much advantage in struggling through every ailment. If he can be
made happy, as you and Helen will, I doubt not, be able
to make him, and kept strictly to a wholesome, natural
country life here, it is not impossible he may live to enter upon his property. And then—for the future, God
knows!"

"It is well for us," replied the minister, gravely, "that
He does know—every thing."

"I suppose it is."

And then for another hour the two good men — one
living in the world and the other out of it—both fathers
of families, carrying their own burden of cares, and having gone through their own personal sorrows each in his
day, talked over, in the minutest degree, the present, and,
so far as they could divine it, the future of this poor boy,
who, through so strange a combination of circumstances,
had been left entirely to their charge.

"It is a most responsible charge, Mr. Cardross, and I

feel almost selfish in shifting it so much from my own shoulders upon yours."

" I am willing to undertake it. Perhaps it may do me good," returned the minister, with a slight sigh.

"And you will give him the best education you can— your own, in short, which is more than sufficient for any Lord Cairnforth; certainly more than the last earl had, or his father either."

"Possibly," said Mr. Cardross, who remembered both —stalwart, active, courtly lords of the soil, great at field-sports and festivities, but not over given to study. "No, the present earl does not take after his progenitors in any way. You should just see him, Mr. Menteith, over his Virgil; and I have promised to begin Homer with him to-morrow. It does one's heart good to see a boy so fond of his books," added the minister, warming up into an enthusiasm which delighted the other extremely.

"Yes, I think my plan was right," said he, rubbing his hands. "It will work well on both sides. There could not be found any where a better tutor than yourself for the earl. He never can go much into the world; he may not even live to be of age; still, as long as he does live, his life ought to be made as pleasant — I mean, as little painful to him as possible. And he ought to be fitted, in case he should live, for as many as he can fulfill of the duties of his position; its enjoyments, alas! he will never know."

"I am not so sure of that," replied Mr. Cardross. "He loves books; he may turn out a thoroughly educated and accomplished student — perhaps even a man of let-ters. To have a thirst for knowledge, and unlimited means to gratify it, is not such a bad thing. Why," continued the minister, glancing round on his own poorly-furnished shelves, where every book was bought almost at the sacrifice of a meal, "he will be rich enough to stock from end to end that wilderness of shelves in the half-finished Castle library. How pleasant that must be!"

Mr. Menteith smiled as if he did not quite comprehend this sort of felicity. "But, in any case, Lord Cairnforth seems to have, what will be quite as useful to him as brains, a very kindly heart. He does not shut himself up in a morbid way, but takes an interest in all about him. Look at him, now, how heartily he is laughing at something your daughter has said. Really, those two seem quite happy."

"Helen makes every body happy," fondly said Helen's father.

"I believe so. I shall be sending down one of my big lads to look after her some day. I've eight of them, Mr. Cardross, all to be educated, settled, and wived. It's a 'sair fecht,' I assure you."

"I know it; but still it has its compensations."

"Ay, they're all strong, likely, braw fellows, who can push their own way in the world and fend for themselves. Not like—" he glanced over to the group on the grass, and stopped. Yet at that moment a hearty trill of thoroughly childish laughter seemed to rebuke the regrets of both fathers.

"That child certainly has the sweetest nature — the most remarkable faculty for enjoying other people's enjoyments, in which he himself can never share."

"Yes, it was always so, from the time he was a mere infant. Dr. Hamilton often noticed it, and said it was a good omen."

"I believe so," rejoined Mr. Cardross, earnestly. "I feel sure that if Lord Cairnforth lives, he will neither have a useless nor an unhappy life."

"Let us hope not. And yet—poor little fellow!—to be the last Earl of Cairnforth, and to be—such as he is!"

"He is what God made him, what God willed him to be," said the minister, solemnly. "We know not why it should be so; we only know that it is, and we can not alter it. We can not remove from him his heavy cross, but I think we can help him to bear it."

"You are a good man, Mr. Cardross," replied the Edinburg writer, huskily, as he rose from his seat, and declining another glass of the claret, of which, under some shallow pretext, he had sent a supply into the minister's empty cellar, he crossed the grass-plot, and spent the rest of the evening beside his ward and Helen.

Chapter the Fifth.

D

DAYS, months, and years slip smoothly by on the shores of Loch Beg. Even now, though the cruelly advancing finger of Civilization has touched it, dotted it with genteel villas on either side, plowed it with smoky steam-boats, and will shortly frighten the innocent fishes by dropping a marine telegraph wire across the mouth of the loch, it is a peaceful place still. But when the last Earl of Cairnforth was a child it was all peace. In summer time a few stray tourists would wander past it, wondering at its beauty; but in winter it had hardly any communication with the outer world. The Manse, the Castle, and the clachan, with a few outlying farm-houses, comprised the whole of Cairnforth; and the little peninsula, surrounded on three sides by water, and on the fourth by hills, was sufficiently impregnable and isolated to cause existence to flow on there very quietly, in what townspeople call dullness, and country people repose.

For, whatever repose there may be in country life—real country—there is certainly no monotony. The perpetual change of seasons, varying the aspect of the outside world every month, every week—nay, almost every day, is a continual interest to observant minds, and especially so to intelligent children, who are as yet lying on the breast of Mother Nature only, nor have begun to feel or understand the darker and sadder interests of human passion and emotion.

The little Earl of Cairnforth was one of these; and many a time, through all the summers of his life, he recalled tenderly that first summer at Cairnforth, when, no longer pent up between walls and roofs, or dragged about in carriages, he learned, by Malcolm's aid and under Helen's teaching, to chronicle time in different ways; first by the hyacinths and primroses vanishing, and giving place to the wild roses—those exquisite deep-red roses which belong especially to this country-side; then by the woods —his own woods—growing fragrant with innumerable honeysuckles; and lastly by the heather on the moorland—Scotland's own flower—which clothes entire hillsides as with a garment of gorgeous purple, and fills the whole atmosphere wtih the scent of a spice-garden; and when it faded into a soft brown, dying delicately, beautiful to the last, there appeared the brambles, trailing every where, with their pretty yellowing leaves and their delicious berries. How blithe, even like a mere "callant," big Malcolm was, when, leaving the earl on the sunny hill-side under Miss Cardross's charge, he used to wander off, and come back with his hands all torn and scratched, to feed his young master with blackberries!

"He is not unhappy—I am sure the child is not unhappy," Helen often said to her father, when—as was his way—Mr. Cardross would get fits of uncertainty and downheartedness, and think he was killing his pupil with study, or wearying him, and risking his health by letting him do as much as his energetic mind, always dominant over the frail body, prompted him to do. "Only let him

love his life, and put as much in it as he can, be it long
or short, and then it will never be a sad life or a life
thrown away."

"Helen, you're not clever, but you're a wise little woman, my dear," the minister would say, patting the flaxen
curls or the busy hands—large and brown, yet with a
certain grace about them, too—helpful hands, made to
hold children, or tend sick folk, or sustain the feeble steps
of old age. She was "no bonnie" Helen Cardross; it
was just a round, rosy, sonsie face, with no features in
particular, but she was pleasant to look upon, and inexpressibly pleasant to live with; for it was such a wholesome nature, so entirely free from moods, or fancies, or
crotchets of any kind—those sad vagaries of ill-health, ill-
humor, and ill-conditionedness of every sort, which are
sometimes only a misfortune, caused by an unhappy natural temperament, but oftener arise from pure egotism,
of which there was not an atom in Helen Cardross. Her
life was like the life of a flower—as natural, unconscious,
fresh, and sweet: she took in every influence about her,
and gave out freely all she had to give; desired no better things than she possessed, and where she was planted
there she grew.

It was not wonderful that the little earl loved her,
and that under her sunshiny soul his life too blossomed
out as it might never otherwise have done, but have
drooped and faded, and gone back into the darkness, imperfect and unfulfilled; for, though each human life is,
in a sense, complete to itself, and must work itself out in-
dependently, clinging to no other, still there is a great
and beautiful mystery in the way one life seems to influ-

encean other, sometimes for ill, but far, far oftener for good.

Lord Cairnforth was not much with the Cardross boys. He liked them, and evidently craved after their company, but they were very shy of him. Sometimes they let Malcolm bring him into their boat, and condescended to row him up and down the loch, a mode of locomotion in which he greatly delighted; for, at best, the shaking of the great lumbering coach was not easy to him, and he always begged to be carried in Malcolm's arms till he found how pleasantly he could lie in the stern of the Manse boat, and float about on the smooth water, watching the mountains and the shores.

True, he could not stir an inch from where he was laid down, but he lay there so contentedly, enjoying every thing, and really looked, what he often said he was, " as happy as a king."

And by degrees, with a little home persuasion from Helen, the boys got reconciled to his company—found, indeed, that he was not such bad company after all; for often, when they were tired of pulling, and let the boat drift into some quiet little bay, or rock lazily in the middle of the loch, the little earl would begin talking—telling stories, which soon caught the attention of the minister's boys. These were either fragments out of the books he had read, which seemed countless to the young Cardrosses, or, what they liked still better, tales "out of his own head;" and these tales were always the last that they would have expected from one like him—wild exploits; wanderings over South American prairies, or shipwrecks on desert islands; astonishing feats of riding, or fighting,

·or traveling by land and sea—every thing, in short, belonging to that sort of active, energetic, adventurous life, of which the relator could never have had the least experience, and never would have in this world. Perhaps for that very reason his fancy delighted therein the more.

: And his stories were enjoyed by others as much as by himself, which no doubt added to the charm of them. When winter came, and all the boating days were done, many a night, round the fire of the Manse parlor, or in the "awful eerie" library at the Castle, the earl used to have a whole circle of young people, and some elder ones too, gathered round his wheel-chair, listening to his wonderful tales of adventure by flood and field.

"Why don't you write them out properly?" the boys would ask sometimes, forgetting—what Helen would never have forgotten. But he only looked down on his poor helpless fingers and smiled.

However, he had, with great difficulty and pains, managed to learn to write—that is, to sign his name, or indite any short letter to Mr. Menteith or others, which, as he grew older, sometimes became necessary. But writing was always a great trouble to him; and, fortunately, people were not expected to write much in those days. Had he been born a little later in his century, the Earl of Cairnforth might have brightened his sad life by putting his imagination forth in print, and becoming a great literary character; as it was, he merely told his tales for his own delight and that of those about him, which possibly was a better thing than fame.

Then he made jokes, too. Sometimes, in his quiet, dry way, he said such droll things that the Cardross boys fell into shouts of laughter. He had the rare quality of seeing the comical side of things, without a particle of ill-nature being mixed up with his fun. His wit danced about as brilliantly and harmlessly as the Northern lights that flashed and flamed of winter nights over the mountains at the head of the loch; and the solid, somewhat heavy Manse boys, gradually growing up to men, often wondered why it was that, miserable as the earl's life was, or seemed to them, they always felt merrier instead of sadder when they were in his company.

But sometimes when with Helen alone, and more especially as he grew to be a youth in his teens, and yet no bigger, no stronger, and scarcely less helpless than a child, the young earl would let fall a word or two which showed that he was fully and painfully aware of his own condition, and of all that it entailed. It was evident that he had thought much and deeply of the future which lay before him. If, as now appeared probable, he should live to man's estate, his life must, at best, be one long endurance, rendered all the sharper and harder to bear because within that helpless body dwelt a soul, which was, more than that of most men, alive to every thing beautiful, noble, active, and good.

However, though he occasionally betrayed these workings of his mind, it was only to Helen, and not to her very much, for he was exceedingly self-contained from his very childhood. He seemed to feel by instinct that to him had been allotted a special solitude of existence, into which, try as tenderly as they would, none could ever fully penetrate, and with which none could wholly sympathize. It was inevitable in the nature of things.

He apparently accepted the fact as such, and did not attempt to break through it. He took the strongest interest in other people, and in every thing around him, but he did not seem to expect to have the like returned in any great degree. Perhaps it was one of those merciful compensations that what he could not have he was made strong enough to do without.

So things went on, without any other variety than an occasional visit from Mr. Menteith or Dr. Hamilton, for seven years, during which the minister's pupil had acquired every possible learning that his teacher could give, and was fast becoming less a scholar than an equal companion and friend—so familiar and dear, that Mr. Cardross, like all who knew him, had long since almost forgotten that the earl was—what he was. It seemed the most natural thing in the world that he should sit there in his little chair, doing nothing; absolutely passive to all physical things; but interested in every thing and every body, and, whether at the Manse or the Castle, as completely one of the circle as if he took the most active part therein. Consulted by one, appealed to by another, joked by a third—he was ever ready with a joke—it was only when strangers happened to see him, and were startled by the sight, that his own immediate friends recognized how different he was from other people.

It was one day when he was about nineteen that Helen, coming in to see him with a message from her father, who wanted to speak to him about some parish matters, found Lord Cairnforth deeply meditating over a letter. He slipped it aside, however, and it was not until the whole parish question had been discussed and settled, as somehow he and Helen very often did settle the whole affairs of the parish between them, that he brought it out again, fidgeting it out of his pocket with his poor fingers, which seemed a little more helpless than usual.

"Helen, I wish you would read that, and tell me what you think about it?"

It was a letter somewhat painful to read, with the earl sitting by and watching her, but Helen had long learned never to shrink from these sort of things. He felt them far less if every body else faced them as boldly as he had himself always done.

The letter was from Dr. Hamilton, written after his return from a three days' visit at Cairnforth Castle. It explained, after a long apologetic preamble, the burden of which was that the earl was now old enough and thoughtful enough to be the best person to speak to on such a difficult subject, that there had been a certain skillful mechanician lately in Edinburg who declared he would invent some support by which Lord Cairnforth could be made, not indeed to walk—that was impossible—but to be by many degrees more active than now. But it would be necessary for him to go to London, and there submit to a great amount of trouble and inconvenience—possibly some pain.

"I tell you this last, my dear lord," continued the good doctor, "because I ought not to deceive you; and because, so far as I have seen, you are a courageous boy— nay, almost a man—or will be soon. I must forewarn you also that the experiment is only an experiment— that it may fail; but even in that case you would be only where you were before—no better, no worse, except for the temporary annoyance and suffering."

"And if it succeeded?" said Helen, almost in a whisper, as she returned the letter.

The earl smiled—a bright, vague, but hopeful smile— "I might be a little more able to do things—to live my life with a little less trouble to myself, and possibly to other people. Well, Helen? You don't speak, but I think your eyes say 'Try!'"

"Yes, my dear." She sometimes, though not often now, lest it might vex him by making him still so much of a child, called him "my dear."

This ended the conversation, which Helen did not communicate to any body, nor referred to again with Lord Cairnforth, though she pondered over it and him continually.

A week after this, Mr. Menteith unexpectedly appeared at the Castle, and after a long consultation with Mr. Cardross, it was agreed that what seemed the evident wish of the earl should be accomplished if possible; that he, Malcolm, Mrs. Campbell, and Mr. Menteith should start for London immediately.

Such a journey was then a very different thing from what it is now, and to so helpless a traveler as Lord Cairnforth its difficulties were doubled. He had to post the whole distance in his own carriage, which was fitted up so as to be as easy as possible in locomotion, besides being so arranged that he could sleep in it if absolutely necessary, for ordinary beds and ordinary chairs were sometimes very painful to him. Had he been born poor, in all probability he would long ago have died—of sheer suffering.

Fortunately it was summer time. He staid at Cairnforth till after his birthday, "for I may never see another," said he, with that gentle smile which seemed to imply that he would be neither glad nor sorry, and then he started. He was quite cheerful himself, but Mr. Menteith and Mrs. Campbell looked very anxious. Malcolm was full of superstitious forebodings, and Helen Cardross and her father, when they bade him good-by, and watched the carriage drive slowly from the Castle doors, felt as sad as if they were parting from him, not for London, but for the other world.

Not until he was gone did they recognize how much they missed him: in the Manse parlor, where "the earl's chair" took its regular place—in the pretty Manse garden, where its wheels had made in the gravel walks deep marks which Helen could not bear to have erased—in his pew at the kirk, where the minister had learned to look Sunday after Sunday for that earnest, listening face. Mr. Cardross, too, found it dull no longer to have his walk up to the Castle, and his hour or two's rest in the yet unfinished library, which he and Lord Cairnforth had already begun to consult about, and where the earl was always to be found, sitting at his little table with his books about him, and Malcolm lurking within call, or else placed contentedly by the French window, looking out upon that blaze of beauty into which the countess's flower-garden had grown. How little they had thought —the young father and mother, cut off in the midst of their plans, that their poor child would one day so keenly enjoy them all, and have such sore need for these or any other simple and innocent enjoyments.

"Papa, how we do miss him!" said Helen one day as

she walked with her father through the Cairnforth woods. "Who would have thought it when he first came here only a few years ago?"

"Who would indeed?" said the minister, remembering a certain walk he had taken through these very paths nineteen years before, when he had wondered why Providence had sent the poor babe into the world at all, and thought how far, far happier it would have been lying dead on its dead mother's bosom—that beautiful young mother, whose placid face upon the white satin pillows of her coffin Mr. Cardross yet vividly recalled; for he saw it often reflected in the living face of the son, whom, happily, she had died without beholding.

"That was a wise saying of King David's, 'Let me fall into the hands of the Lord, and not into the hands of men,'" mused Mr. Cardross, who had just been hearing from Mr. Menteith a long story of his perplexities with "those Bruces," and had also had lately a few domestic dissensions in his own parish, which did quarrel among itself occasionally, and always brought its quarrels to be settled by the minister. "It is a strange thing, Helen, my dear, what wonderful peace there often is in great misfortunes. They are quite different from the petty miseries which people make for themselves."

"I suppose so. But do you think, papa, that any good will come out of this London journey?"

"I can not tell; still, it was right to try. You yourself said it was right to try."

"Yes;" and then, seeing it was done now, the practical, brave Helen stilled her uncertainties and let the matter rest.

No one was surprised that weeks elapsed before there came any tidings of the travelers. Then Mr. Menteith wrote, announcing their safe arrival in London, which diffused great joy throughout the parish, for of course every body knew whither Lord Cairnforth had gone, and many knew the reason why. Scarcely a week passed that some of the far-distant tenantry even, who lived on the other side of the peninsula, did not cross the hills, walking many miles for no reason but to ask at the Manse what was the latest news of "our earl."

But after the first letter there came no farther tidings, and indeed none were expected. Mr. Menteith had probably returned to Edinburg, and in those days there was no penny post, and nobody indulged in unnecessary correspondence. Still, sometimes Helen thought, with a sore uneasiness, "If the earl had had good news to tell, he would have surely told it. He was always so glad to make any body happy."

The long summer twilights were ended, and one or two equinoctial gales had whipped the waters of Loch Beg into wild "white horses," yet still Lord Cairnforth did not return. At last, one Monday night, when Helen and her father were returning from a three days' absence at the "preachings"—that is, the half-yearly sacrament— in a neighboring parish, they saw, when they came to the ferry, the glimmer of lights from the Castle windows on the opposite shore of the loch.

" I do believe Lord Cairnforth is come home !"

" Ou ay, Miss Helen," said Duncan, the ferryman, "his lordship crossed wi' me the day; an' I'm thinking, minister," added the old man, confidentially, "that ye suld

just gang up to the Castle an' see him ; for it's ma opinion that the earl's come back as he gaed awa, nae better
and nae waur."

"What makes you think so ? Did he say any thing?"

"Ne'er a word but just ' How are ye the day, Duncan?'
and he sat and glowered at the hills and the loch, and
twa big draps rolled down his puir bit facie—it's grown
sae white and sae sma', ye ken—and I said, 'My lord,
it's grand to see your lordship back. Ye'll no be gaun
to London again, I hope?' 'Na, na,' says he ; 'na, Duncan, I'm best at hame—best at hame!' And when Malcolm lifted him, he gied a bit skreigh, as if he'd hurted
himsel—Minister, I wish I'd thae London doctors here
by our loch side," muttered Duncan between his teeth,
and pulling away fiercely at his oar ; but the minister
said nothing.

He and Helen went silently home, and finding no message, walked on as silently up to the Castle together.

Chapter the Sixth.

OLD Duncan's penetration had been correct—the diffi-cult and painful London journey was all in vain. Lord Cairnforth had returned home neither better nor worse than he was before: the experiment had failed.

Helen and her father guessed this from their first sight of him, though they had found him sitting as usual in his arm-chair at his favorite corner, and when they en-tered the library he had looked up with a smile — the same old smile, as natural as though he had never been away.

"Is that you, Mr. Cardross? Helen too? How very kind of you to come and see me so soon!"

But, in spite of his cheerful greeting, they detected at once the expression of suffering in the poor face—"sae white and sae sma'," as Duncan had said; pale beyond its ordinary pallor, and shrunken and withered like an old man's; the more so, perhaps, as the masculine down had grown upon cheek and chin, and there was a ma-tured manliness of expression in the whole countenance, which formed a strange contrast to the still puny and childish frame—alas! not a whit less helpless or less dis-torted than before. Yes, the experiment had failed.

They were so sure of this, Mr. Cardross and his daugh-ter, that neither put to him a single question on the subject, but instinctively passed it over, and kept the conversation to all sorts of commonplace topics: the journey —the wonders of London—and the small events which had happened in quiet Cairnforth during the three months that the earl had been away.

Lord Cairnforth was the first to end their difficulty and hesitation by openly referring to that which neither of his friends could bear to speak of.

"Yes," he said, at last, with a faint, sad smile, "I agree with old Duncan—I never mean to go to London any more. I shall stay for the rest of my days among my own people."

"So much the better for them," observed the minister, warmly.

"Do you think that? Well, we shall see. I must try and make it so, as well as I can. I am but where I was before, as Dr. Hamilton said. Poor Dr. Hamilton! he is so sorry."

Mr. Cardross did not ask about what, but turned to the table and began cutting open the leaves of a book. For Helen, she drew nearer to Lord Cairnforth's chair, and laid over the poor, weak, wasted fingers her soft, warm hand.

The tears sprang to the young earl's eyes. "Don't speak to me," he whispered; "it is all over now; but it was very hard for a time."

"I know it."

"Yes—at least as much as you can know."

Helen was silent. She recognized, as she had never recognized before, the awful individuality of suffering which it had pleased God to lay upon this one human being — suffering at which even the friends who loved him best could only stand aloof and gaze, without the possibility of alleviation.

" Ay," he said, at last, "it is all over: I need try no more experiments. I shall just sit still and be content."

What was the minute history of the experiments he had tried, how much bodily pain they had cost him, and through how much mental pain he had struggled before he attained that "content," he did not explain even to Helen. He turned the conversation to the books which Mr. Cardross was cutting, and many other books, of which he had bought a whole cart-load for the minister's library. Neither then, nor at any other time, did he ever refer, except in the most cursory way, to his journey to London.

But Helen noticed that for a long while—weeks, nay, months, he seemed to avoid more than ever any conversation about himself. He was slightly irritable and uncertain of mood, and disposed to shut himself up in the Castle, reading, or seeming to read, from morning till night. It was not till a passing illness of the minister's in some degree forced him that he reappeared at the Manse, and fell into his old ways of coming and going, resuming his studies with Mr. Cardross, and his walks with Helen — or rather drives, for he had ceased to be carried in Malcolm's arms.

"I am a man now, or ought to be," he said once, as a reason for this, after which no one made any remarks on the subject. Malcolm still retained his place as the earl's close attendant—as faithful as his shadow, almost as silent.

But the next year or so made a considerable alteration in Lord Cairnforth. Not in growth—the little figure never grew any bigger than that of a boy of ten or twelve; but the childish softness passed from the face; it sharpened, and hardened, and became that of a young man. The features developed; and a short black beard, soft and curly, for it had never known the razor, added character to what, in ordinary men, would have been considered a very handsome face. It had none of the painful expression so often seen in deformed persons, but more resembled those sweet Italian heads of youthful saints—Saint Sebastian's, for instance—which the old masters were so fond of painting; and though there was a certain melancholy about it when in repose, during conversation it brightened up, and was the cheerfullest, most sunshiny face imaginable.

That is, it ultimately became so; but for a long time after the journey to London a shadow hung over it, which rarely quite passed away except in Helen's company. Nobody could be dreary for long beside Helen Cardross; and either through her companionship, or his own inherent strength of will, or both combined, the earl gradually recovered from the bitterness of lost hopes, whatsoever they had been, and became once more his own natural self, perhaps even more cheerful, since it was now not so much the gayety of a boy as the composed, equable serenity of a thoughtful man.

His education might be considered complete: it had advanced to the utmost limit to which Mr. Cardross could carry it; but the pupil insisted on retaining, nominally and pecuniarily, his position at the Manse.

Or else the two would spend hours—nay, days, shut up together in the Castle library, the beautiful octagon room, with its painted ceiling, and its eight walls lined from floor to roof with empty shelves, to plan the filling of which was the delight of the minister's life, since, but for his poor parish and his large family, Mr. Cardross would have been a thorough bibliomaniac. Now, in a vicarious manner, the hobby of his youth reappeared, and at every cargo of books that arrived at the Castle his old eyes brightened—for he was growing to look really an old man now—and he would plunge among them with an ardor that sometimes made both the earl and Helen smile. But Helen's eyes were dim too, for she saw through all the tender cunning, and often watched Lord Cairnforth as he sat contentedly in his little chair, in the midst of a pile of books, examining, directing, and sympathizing, though doing nothing. Alas! nothing could he do. But it was one of the secrets which made these three lives so peaceful, that each could throw itself out of itself into that of another, and take thence, secondarily, the sunshine that was denied to its own.

Beyond the family at the Manse the earl had no acquaintance whatsoever, and seemed to desire none. His rank lifted him above the small proprietors who lived within visitable distance of the Castle: they never attempted to associate with him. Sometimes a stray caller appeared, prompted by curiosity, which Mrs. Campbell generally found ingenious reasons for leaving ungratified, and Lord Cairnforth's excessive shyness and dislike to appear before strangers did the rest. It is astonishing how little the world cares to cultivate those out of whom it can get nothing; and the small establishment at Cairnforth Castle, with its almost invisible head, soon ceased to be an object of interest to any body—at least to any body in that sphere of life where the earl would other- wise have moved.

Among his own tenantry, the small farmers along the shores of the two lochs which bounded the peninsula, his long minority and mysterious affliction made him person- ally almost unknown. They used to come twice a year, at Whitsunday and Martinmas, to pay their rents to Mr. Menteith; to inquire for my lord's health, and to drink it in abundance of whisky; but the earl himself they never saw, and their feelings toward him were a mixture of reverence and awe.

It was different with the earl's immediate neighbors, the humble inhabitants of the clachan. These, during the last nine years, had gradually grown familiar, first with the little childish form, carried about tenderly in Malcolm's arms, and then with the muffled figure, scarce- ly less of a child to look at, which Malcolm, and some- times Miss Cardross, drove about in a pony-chaise. At the kirk especially, though he was always carefully con- veyed in first, and borne out last of all the congregation, his face—his sweet, kind, beautiful face was known to them all, and the children were always taught to doff their bonnets or pull their forelocks to the earl.

Beyond that, nobody knew any thing about him. His large property, accumulating every year, was entirely un- der the management of Mr. Menteith; he himself took no interest in it; and the way by which the former heirs of Cairnforth had used to make themselves popular from boyhood, by going among the tenantry, hunting, shoot- ing, fishing, and boating, was impossible to this earl. His distant dependents hardly remembered his existence, and he took no heed of theirs, until a few months before he came of age, when one of these slight chances which often determine so much changed the current of affairs.

It was just before the "term." Mr. Menteith had been expected all day, but had not arrived, and the earl had taken a long drive with Helen and her father through the Cairnforth woods, where the wild daffodils were beginning to succeed the fading snowdrops, and the mavises had been heard to sing those few rich notes which belong especially to the twilights of early spring, an earnest of all the richness, and glory, and delight of the year. The little party seemed to feel it—that soft, dreamy sense of dawning spring, which stirs all the soul, especially in youth, with a vague looking forward to some pleasantness which never comes. They sat, silent and talking by turns, beside the not unwelcome fire, in a corner of the large library.

"We shall miss Alick a good deal this spring," said Helen, recurring to a subject of which the family heart was full, the departure of the eldest son to "begin the world" in Mr. Menteith's office in Edinburg. He was not a very clever lad, but he was sensible and steady, and blessed with that practical mother-wit which is often better than brains. The minister, though he had been bemoaning his boy's "little Latin and less Greek," and comparing Alick's learning very disadvantageously with that of the earl, to whom Mr. Cardross confided all his troubles, nevertheless seemed both proud and hopeful of his eldest son, the heir to his honest name, which Alick would now carry out into a far wider world than that of

E

the poor minister of Cairnforth, and doubtless, in good
time, transmit honorably to a third generation.

"Yes," added the father, when innumerable castles in
the air had been built and rebuilt for Alick's future, "I'll
not deny that my lad is a good lad. He is the hope of
the house, and he knows it. It's little of worldly gear
that he'll get for many a day, and he tells me he will
have to work from morning till night; but he rather enjoys the prospect than not."

"No wonder. Work must be a happy thing," said,
with a sigh, the young Earl of Cairnforth.

Helen's heart smote her for having let the conversation
drift into this direction, as it did occasionally, when, from
their long familiarity with him, they forgot how he must
feel about many things, natural enough to them, but to
him, unto whom the outer world, with all its duties, energies, enjoyments, could never be any thing but a name,
full of sharpest pain. She said, after a few minutes
watching of the grave, still face—not exactly sad, but
only very still, very grave—

"Just look at papa, how happy he is among those
books you sent for! Your plan of his arranging the
library is the delight of his life."

"Is it? I am so glad," said the earl, brightening up
at once. "What a good thing I thought of it!"

"You always do think of every thing that is good
and kind," said Helen, softly.

"Thank you," and the shadow passed away, as any
trifling pleasure always had power to make it pass.
Sometimes Helen speculated vaguely on what a grand
sort of man the earl would have been had he been like

other people — how cheerful, how active, how energetic and wise. But then one never knows how far circum stances create and unfold character. We often learn as much by what is withheld as by what is enjoyed.

"Helen," he said, moving his chair a little nearer her —he had brought one good thing from London, a self acting chair, in which he could wheel himself about easi ly, and liked doing it — "I wonder whether your father would have taken as much pleasure in his books thirty years ago. Do you think one could fill up one's whole life with reading and study?"

"I can not say; I'm not clever myself, you know."

"Oh, but you are—with a sort of practical cleverness. And so is Alick, in his own way. How happy Alick must be, going out into the world, with plenty to do all day long! How bright he looked this morning!"

"He sees only the sunny side of things; he is still no more than a boy."

"Not exactly; he is a year older than I am."

Helen hardly knew what to reply. She guessed so well the current of the earl's thoughts, which were often her own too, as she watched his absent or weary looks, though he tried hard to keep his attention to what Mr. Cardross was reading or discussing. But the distance between twenty and sixty — the life beginning and the life advancing toward its close — was frequently appar ent; also between an active, original mind, requiring hu manity for its study, and one whose whole bent was among the dry bones of ancient learning—the difference, in short, between learning and knowledge—the mere stu dent and the man who only uses study as a means to the perfecting of his whole nature, his complete existence as a human being.

All this Helen felt with her quick, feminine instinct, but she did not clearly understand it, and she could not reason about it at all. She only answered in a troubled sort of way that she thought every body, somehow or other, might in time find enough to do — to be happy in doing — and she was trying to put her meaning into more connected and intelligible form, when, greatly to her relief, Malcolm entered the library.

Malcolm, being so necessary and close a personal attendant on the earl, always came and went about his master without any body's noticing him; but now Helen fancied he was making signals to her or to some one. Lord Cairnforth detected them.

"Is any thing wrong, Malcolm? Speak out; don't hide things from me. I am not a child now."

There was just the slightest touch of sharpness in the gentle voice, and Malcolm did speak out.

"I wadna be troubling ye, my lord, but it's just an auld man, Dougal Mac Dougal, frae the head o' Loch Mhor—a puir doited body, wha says he maun hae a bit word wi' your lordship. But I tellt him ye couldna be fashed wi' the likes o' him."

"That was not civil or right, Malcolm — an old man, too. Where is he?"

"Just by the door—eh—and he's coming ben—the ill-mannered loon!" cried Malcolm, angrily, as he interrupted the intruder—a tall, gaunt figure wrapped in a shepherd's plaid, with the bonnet set upon the grizzled head in that sturdy independence — nay, more than independence — rudeness, rough and thorny as his own thistle, which is the characteristic of the Scotch peasant exter- nally, till you get below the surface to the warm, kindly heart.

"I'm no ill-mannered, and I'll just gang through the hale house till I find my lord," said the old man, shaking off Malcolm with a strength that his seventy odd years seemed scarcely to have diminished. "I'm wushing nae harm to ony o' ye, but I maun get speech o' my lord. He's no a bairn; he'll be ane-and-twenty the thirtieth o' June: I mind the day weel, for the wife was brought to bed o' her last wean the same day as the countess, and our Dougal's a braw callant the noo, ye ken. Gin the earl has ony wits ava, whilk folk thocht was aye doubt- fu', he'll hae gotten them by this time. I maun speak wi' himsel', unless, as they said, he's no a' there."

"Haud your tongue, ye fule!" cried Malcolm, stopping him with a fierce whisper. "Yon's my lord!"

The old shepherd started back, for at this moment a sudden blaze-up of the fire showed him, sitting in the cornet, the diminutive figure, attired carefully after the then fashion of gentlemen's dress, every thing rich and complete, even to the black silk stockings and shoes on the small, useless feet, and the white ruffles half hiding the twisted wrists and deformed hands.

"Yes, I am the Earl of Cairnforth. What did you want to say to me?"

He was so bewildered, the rough shepherd, who had spent all his life on the hill-sides, and never seen or imag- ined so sad a sight as this, that at first he could not find a word. Then he said, hanging back and speaking confusedly and humbly, "I ask your pardon, my lord—I didna ken—I'll no trouble ye the day."

"But you do not trouble me at all. Mr. Menteith is not here yet, and I know nothing about business; still, if you wished to speak to me, do so; I am Lord Cairn-forth."

"Are ye?" said the shepherd, evidently bewildered still, so that he forgot his natural awe for his feudal superior. "Are ye the countess's bairn, that's just the age o' our Dougal? Dougal's ane o' the gamekeepers, ye ken —sic a braw fellow—sax feet three. Ye'll hae seen him, maybe?"

"No, but I should like to see him. And yourself—are you a tenant of mine, and what did you want with me?"

Encouraged by the kindly voice, and his own self-interest becoming prominent once more, old Dougal told his tale—not an uncommon one—of sheep lost on the hill-side, and one misfortune following another, until a large family, children and orphan grandchildren, were driven at last to want the "sup o' parritch" for daily food, sinking to such depths of poverty as the earl in his secluded life had never even heard of. And yet the proud old fellow asked nothing except the remission of one year's rent, after having paid rent honestly for half a lifetime. That stolid, silent endurance, which makes a Scotch beggar of any sort about the last thing you ever meet with in Scotland, supported him to the very end.

The earl was deeply touched. As a matter of course, he promised all that was desired of him, and sent the old shepherd away happy; but long after Dougal's departure he sat thoughtful and grave.

"Can such things be, Helen, and I never heard of them? Are some of my people—they are my people, since the land belongs to me—as terribly poor as that man?"

"Ay, very many, though papa looks after them as much as he can. Dougal is out of his parish, or he would have known him. Papa knows every body, and takes care of every body, as far as possible."

"So ought I—or I must do it when I am older," said the earl, thoughtfully.

"There will be no difficulty about that when you come of age and enter on your property."

"Is it a very large property? for I never heard or inquired."

"Very large."

"Show me its boundary; there is the map."

Helen took it down and drew with a pencil the limits of the Cairnforth estates. They extended along the whole peninsula, and far up into the main land.

"There, Lord Cairnforth, every bit of this is yours."

"To do exactly what I like with?"

"Certainly."

"Helen, it is an awfully serious thing."

Helen was silent.

"How strange!" he continued, after a pause. "And this was really all mine from the very hour of my birth?"

"Yes."

"And when I come of age I shall have to take my property into my own hands, and manage it just as I choose, or as I can?"

"Of course you will; and I think you can do it, if you try."

For it was not the first time that Helen had pondered over these things, since, being neither learned nor poetical, worldly-minded nor selfish, in her silent hours her mind generally wandered to the practical concerns of other people, and especially of those she loved.

"'Try' ought to be the motto of the Cardross arms— of yours certainly," said Lord Cairnforth, smiling. "I should like to assume it on mine, instead of my own 'Virtute et fide,' which is of little use to me. How can I —*I*—be brave or faithful?"

"You can be both—and you will," said Helen, softly. Years from that day she remembered what she had said, and how true it was.

A little while afterward, while the minister still remained buried in his beloved books, Lord Cairnforth recurred again to Dougal Mac Dougal.

"The old fellow was right. If I am ever to have 'ony wits ava,' I ought to have them by this time. I am nearly twenty-one. Any other young man would have been a man long ago. And I will be a man—why should I not? True manliness is not solely outside. I dare say you could find many a fool and a coward six feet high."

"Yes," answered Helen, all she could find to say.

"And if I have nothing else, I have brains—quite as good brains, I think, as my neighbors. They can not say of me now that I'm 'no a' there.' Nay, Helen, don't look so fierce; they meant me no ill; it was but natural. Yes, God has left me something to be thankful for."

The earl lifted his head—the only part of his frame which he could move freely, and his eyes flashed under his broad brows. Thoroughly manly brows they were, wherein any acute observer might trace that clear sound sense, active energy, and indomitable perseverance which make the real man, and lacking which the "brawest" young fellow alive is a mere body—an animal wanting the soul.

"I wonder how I should set about managing my property. The duty will not be as easy for me as for most people, you know," added he, sadly; "still, if I had a secretary—a thorough man of business, to teach me all about business, and to be constantly at my side, perhaps I might be able to accomplish it. And I might drive about the country—driving is less painful to me now—and get acquainted with my people; see what they wanted, and how I could best help them. They would get used to me, too. I might turn out to be a very respectable laird, and become interested in the improvement of my estates."

"There is great opportunity for that, I know," replied Helen. And then she told him of a conversation she had heard between her father and Mr. Menteith, when the latter had spoken of great changes impending over quiet Cairnforth: how a steamer was to begin plying up and down the loch —how there were continual applications for land to be feued — and how all these improvements would of necessity require the owner of the soil to take many a step unknown to and undreamed of by his forefathers — to make roads, reclaim hill and moorland, build new farms, churches, and school-houses.

"In short, as Mr. Menteith said, the world is changing so fast that the present Earl of Cairnforth will have any thing but the easy life of his father and grandfather."

E 2

"Did Mr. Menteith say that?" cried the earl, eagerly.

"He did, indeed; I heard him."

"And did he seem to think that I should be able for it?"

"I can not tell," answered truthful Helen. "He said not a word one way or the other about your being capable of doing the work; he only said the work was to be done."

"Then I will try and do it."

The earl said this quietly enough, but his eyes gleamed and his lips quivered.

Helen laid her hand upon his, much moved. "I said you were brave — always; still, you must think twice about it, for it will be a very responsible duty—enough, Mr. Menteith told papa, to require a man's whole energies for the next twenty years."

"I wonder if I shall live so long. Well, I am glad, Helen. It will be something worth living for."

Chapter the Seventh.

MALCOLM'S saying that "if my lord taks a thing into his heid he'll aye do't, ye ken," was as true now as when the earl was a little boy.

Mr. Menteith hardly knew how the thing was accomplished—indeed, he had rather opposed it, believing the mere physical impediments to his ward's overlooking his own affairs were insurmountable; but Lord Cairnforth contrived in the course of a day or two to initiate himself very fairly in all the business attendant upon the "term;" to find out the exact extent and divisions of his property, and to whom it was feued. And on term-day he proposed, though with an evident effort which touched the old lawyer deeply, to sit beside Mr. Menteith while the tenants were paying their rents, so as to become personally known to each of them.

Many of these, like Dougal Mac Dougal, were overcome with surprise, nay, something more painful than surprise, at the sight of the small figure which was the last descendant of the noble Earls of Cairnforth, and with whom the stalwart father and the fair young mother, looking down from the pictured walls, contrasted so piteously; but after the first shock was over they carried away only the remembrance of his sweet, grave face, and his intelligent and pertinent observations, indicating

a shrewdness for which even Mr. Menteith was unpre-
pared. When he owned this, after business was done,
the young earl smiled, evidently much gratified.

"Yes, I don't think they can say of me that I'm 'no a'
there!'" Also he that evening confessed to Helen that
he found "business" nearly as interesting as Greek and
Latin, perhaps even more so, for there was something
human in it, something which drew one closer to one's
fellow-creatures, and benefited other people besides one's
self. "I think," he added, "I should rather enjoy being
what is called 'a good man of business.'"

He pleaded so hard for farther instruction in all per-
taining to his estate that Mr. Menteith consented to spare
two whole weeks out of his busy Edinburg life, during
which Lord Cairnforth and he were shut up together for
a great part of every day, investigating matters connected with the property, and other things which hitherto in
the young man's education had been entirely neglected.

"For," said his guardian, sadly, "I own, I never
thought of him as a young man—or as a man at all;
nevertheless, he is one, and will always be. That clear,
cool head of his, just for brains, pure brains, is worth both
his father's and grandfather's put together."

And when Helen repeated this saying to Lord Cairn-·
forth, he smiled his exceedingly bright smile, and was
more than cheerful, joyous, for days after.

On Mr. Menteith's return home, he sent back to the
Castle one of his old clerks, who had been acquainted
with the Cairnforth affairs for nearly half a century; he
also was astonished at the capacity which the young earl
showed. Of course, physically, he was entirely helpless;

the little forked stick was still in continual requisition;
nor could he write except with much difficulty; but he .
had the faculty of arrangement and order, and the rare
power—rarer than is supposed—of guiding and govern-
ing, so that what he could not do himself he could direct
others how to do, and thus attain his end so perfectly,
that even those who knew him best were oftentimes actually amazed at the result he effected.

Then he enjoyed his work; took such an interest in
the plans for feuing land along the loch-side, and the sort
of houses that was to be built upon each feu, the roads
he would have to make, and especially in the grand
wooden pier which, by Mr. Menteith's advice, was shortly to be erected in lieu of the little quay of stones at the
ferry, which had hitherto served as Cairnforth's chief link
with the outside world.

If Mr. Cardross and Helen grieved a little over this advancing tide of civilization, which might soon sweep away
many things old and dear from the shores of beautiful
Loch Beg, they grew reconciled when they saw the light
in the earl's eyes, and heard him talk with an interest
and enthusiasm quite new to him of what he meant to do
when he came of age. Only in all his projects was one
peculiarity rather uncommon in young heirs—the entire
absence of any schemes for personal pleasure. Comforts
he had, of course; his faithful friends and servants took
care that his condition should have every alleviation that
wealth could furnish; but of enjoyments, after the fashion of youth, he planned nothing; for, indeed, what of
them was left him to enjoy?

And so, faster than usual, being so well filled with occupations, the weeks and months slipped by, until the important thirtieth of June, when Mr. Menteith's term of guardianship would end, and a man's free life and independent duties, so far as he could perform them, would legally begin for the Earl of Cairnforth.

There had been great consultations on this topic all along the two lochs, and beyond them, for Dougal Mac Dougal had carried his story of the earl and his goodness to the extreme verge of the Cairnforth territory. Throughout June the Manse was weekly haunted by tenants arriving from all quarters to consult the minister, the universal referee, as to how best they could celebrate the event, which, whenever it occurred, had for generations been kept gloriously in the little peninsula, though no case was known of any earl's attaining his majority as being already Earl of Cairnforth. The Montgomeries were usually a long-lived race, and their heirs rarely came to their titles till middle-aged fathers of families.

"But we maun hae grand doings this time, ye ken," said an old farmer to the minister, "for I doubt there'll ne'er be anither Earl o' Cairnforth."

Which fact every one seemed sorrowfully to recognize. It was not only probable, but right, that in this Lord Cairnforth—so terribly afflicted—the long line should end.

As the day of the earl's majority approached, the minister's feelings were of such a mingled kind that he shrank from these demonstrations of joy, and rather repressed the warm loyalty which was springing up every where toward the young man. But after taking counsel with Helen, who saw into things a little deeper than he did, Mr. Cardross decided that it was better all should be done exactly as if the present lord were not different from his forefathers, and that he should be helped both to act and to feel as like other people as possible.

Therefore, on a bright June morning, as bright as that of his sad birth-day and his mother's death-day, twenty-one years before, the earl awoke to the sound of music playing—if the national pipes of the peninsula could be called music—underneath his window, and heard his good neighbors from the clachan, young and old, men, women, and bairns, uniting their voices in one hearty shout, wishing "A lang life and a merry ane" to the Earl of Cairnforth.

Whether or not the young man's heart echoed the wish, who could tell? It was among the solemn secrets which every human soul has to keep, and ever must keep, between itself and its Maker.

Very soon the earl appeared out of doors, wheeling himself along the terrace in his little chair, answering smilingly the congratulations of every body, and evidently enjoying the pleasant morning, the sunshine, and the scent of the flowers in what was still called "the countess's garden." People noticed afterward how very like he looked that day to his beautiful mother; and many a mother out of the clachan, who remembered the lady's face still, and how, during her few brief months of married happiness and hope, she used to stop her pretty pony-carriage to notice every poor woman's baby she chanced to pass—many of these now regarded pitifully and tenderly her only son, the last heir of the last Countess of Cairnforth.

Yet he certainly enjoyed himself, there could be no doubt of it; and when, later in the day, he discovered a conspiracy between the Castle, the Manse, and the clach-an, which resulted in a grand feast on the lawn, he was highly delighted.

"All this for me!" he cried, almost childish in his pleasure. "How good every body is to me!"

And he insisted on mixing with the little crowd, and seeing them sit down to their banquet, which they ate as if they had never eaten in their lives before, and drank —as Highlanders can drink, and Highlanders alone. But, before the whisky began to grow dangerous, the oldest man among the tenantry, who declared that he could remember three Earls of Cairnforth, proposed the health of this earl, which was received with acclamations long and loud, the pipers playing the family tune of "Montgomerie's Reel," which was chiefly notable for hav-ing neither beginning, middle, nor ending.

Lord Cairnforth bowed his head in acknowledgment.

"Ought not somebody to make a little speech of thanks to them?" whispered he to Helen Cardross, who stood close behind his chair.

"You should; and I think you could," was her an-swer.

"Very well; I will try."

And in his poor feeble voice, which trembled much, yet was distinct and clear, he said a few words, very short and simple, to the people near him. He thanked them for all this merry-making in his honor, and said "he was exceedingly happy that day." He told them he meant always to reside at Cairnforth, and to carry out all sorts of plans for the improvement of his estates, both for his tenants' benefit and his own. That he hoped to be both a just and kind landlord, working with and for his tenantry to the utmost of his power.

"That is," he added, with a slight fall of the voice, "to the utmost of those few powers which it has pleased Heaven to give me."

After this speech there was a full minute's silence, tender, touching silence, and then arose a cheer, long and loud, such as had rarely echoed through the little peninsula on the coming of age of any Lord Cairnforth.

When the tenantry had gone away to light bonfires on the hill-side, and perform many other feats of jubilation, a little dinner-party assembled in the large dining-room, which had been so long disused, for the earl always preferred the library, which was on a level with his bedroom, whence he could wheel himself in and out as he pleased. To-day the family table was outspread, and the family plate glittered, and the family portraits stared down from the wall as the last Earl of Cairnforth moved —or rather was moved—slowly down the long room. Malcolm was wheeling him to a side seat well sheltered and comfortable, when he said,

"Stop! Remember I am twenty-one to-day. I think I ought to take my seat at the head of my own table."

Malcolm obeyed. And thus, for the first time since the late earl's death, the place—the master's place—was filled.

"Mr. Cardross, will you say grace?"

The minister tried once—twice—thrice; but his voice failed him. His tender heart, which had lived through so many losses, and this day saw all the past brought before him vivid as yesterday, entirely broke down. Thereupon the earl, from his seat at the head of his own table, repeated simply and naturally the few words which every head of a household—as priest in his own family—may well say, " For these and all other mercies, Lord, make us thankful." ·

After that, Mr. Mentieth took snuff vehemently, and Mr. Cardross openly wiped his eyes. But Helen's, if not quite dry, were very bright. Her woman's heart, which looked beyond the pain of suffering into the beauty of suffering nobly endured, even as faith looks through " the grave and gate of death" into the glories of immortality—Helen's heart was scarcely sad, but very glad and proud.

The day after Lord Cairnforth's coming of age Mr. Menteith formally resigned his trust. He had managed the property so successfully during the long minority that even he himself was surprised at the amount of money, both capital and income, which the earl was now master of, without restriction or reservation, and free from the control of any human being.

" Yes, my lord," said he, when the young man seemed subdued and almost overcome by the extent of his own wealth, "it is really all your own. You may make ducks and drakes of it, as the saying goes, as soon as ever you please. You are accountable for it to no one—except One," added the good, honest, religious man, now growing an old man, and a little gentler, graver, as well as a little more demonstrative than he had been twenty years before.

" Except One. I know that; I hope I shall never forget it," replied the Earl of Cairnforth.

And then they proceeded to wind up their business
affairs.

" How strange it is," observed the earl, when they had
nearly concluded, " how very strange that I should be
here in the world, an isolated human being, with not a
single blood relation, not a soul who has any real claim
upon me !"

" Certainly not—no claim whatsoever; and yet you
are not quite without blood relations."

Lord Cairnforth looked surprised. " I always under-
stood that I had no near kindred."

" Of near kindred you have none. But there are certain far-away cousins, of whom, for many reasons, I never
told you, and begged Mr. Cardross not to tell you either."

" I think I ought to have been told."

Mr. Mentieth explained his strong reasons for silence,
such as the late lord's unpleasant experience—and his
own—of the Bruce family, and the necessity he saw for
keeping his ward quite out of their association and their
influence till his character was matured, and he was of an
age to judge for himself, and act for himself, concerning
them. All the more, because, remote as their kinship
was, and difficult to be proved, still, if proved, they would
be undoubtedly his next heirs.

" My next heirs," repeated the earl—" of course. I
must have an heir. I wonder I never thought of that.
If I died, there must be somebody to succeed me in the
title and estates."

" Not in the title," said Mr. Menteith, hesitating, for he

saw it was opening a subject most difficult and painful, yet which must be opened some time or other, and the old man was too honest to shrink from so doing, if necessary.

"Why not the title?"

"It is entailed, and can be inherited in the direct male line only."

"That is, it descends from father to son?"

"Exactly so."

"I see," said the young man, after a long pause. "Then I am the last Earl of Cairnforth."

There was no answer. Mr. Menteith could not for his life have given one; besides, none seemed required. The earl said it as if merely stating a fact beyond which there is no appeal, and neither expecting nor desiring any refutation or contradiction.

"Now," Lord Cairnforth continued, suddenly changing the conversation, "let us speak once more of the Bruces, who, you say, might any day succeed to my fortune, and would probably make a very bad use of it."

"I believe so; upon my conscience I do!" said Mr. Menteith, earnestly, "else I never should have felt justified in keeping them out of your way as I have done."

"Who are they? I mean, of what does the family consist?"

"An old man—Colonel Bruce he calls himself, and is known as such in every disreputable gambling town on the Continent; a long tribe of girls, and one son, eldest or youngest, I forget which, who was sent to India through some influence I used for your father's sake, but who may be dead by now for aught I know. Indeed,

the utmost I have had to do with the family of late years
has been paying the annuity granted them by the late
earl, which I continued, not legally, but through charity,
on trust that the present earl would never call me to account for the same."

"Most certainly I never shall."

"Then you will take my advice, and forgive my in-
truding upon you a little more of it?"

"Forgive? I am thankful, my good old friend, for
every wise word you say to me."

Again the good lawyer hesitated: "There is a subject,
one exceedingly difficult to speak of, but it should be
named, since you might not think of it yourself. Lord
Cairnforth, the only way in which you can secure your
property against these Bruces is by at once making your
will."

"Making my will!" replied the earl, looking as if the
new responsibilities opening upon him were almost be-
wildering.

"Every man who has any thing to leave ought to
make a will as soon as ever he comes of age. Vainly I
urged this upon your father."

"My poor father! That he should die—so young and
strong—and I should live—how strange it seems! You
think, then—perhaps Dr. Hamilton also thinks—that my
life is precarious?"

"I can not tell; my dear lord, how could any man
possibly tell?"

"Well, it will not make me die one day sooner or later
to have made my will: as you say, every man ought to
do it: I ought especially, for my life is more doubtful

than most people's; and it is a solemn charge to possess so large a fortune as mine."

" Yes. The good—or harm—that might be done with it is incalculable."

"I feel that—at least I am beginning to feel it."

And for a time the earl sat silent and thoughtful; the old lawyer fussing about, putting papers and *débris* of all sorts into their right places, but feeling it awkward to resume the conversation.

" Mr. Menteith, are you at liberty now? for I have quite made up my mind. This matter of the will shall be settled at once. It can be done?"

" Certainly."

" Sit down, then, and I will dictate it. But first you must promise not to interfere with any disposition I may see fit to make of my property."

"I should not have the slightest right to do so, Lord Cairnforth."

" My good old friend! Well, now, how shall we begin?"

"I should recommend your first stating any legacies you may wish to leave to dependents—for instance, Mrs. Campbell, or Malcolm, and then bequeathing the whole bulk of your estates to some one person—some young person likely to outlive you, and upon whom you can depend to carry out all your plans and intentions, and make as good a use of your fortune as you would have done yourself. That is my principle as to choice of an heir. There are many instances in which blood is *not* thicker than water, and a friend by election is often worthier and dearer, besides being closer than any relative."

"You are right."

"Still, consanguinity must be considered a little. You might leave a certain sum to these Bruces—or if, on inquiry, you found among them any child whom you approved, you could adopt him as your heir, and he could take the name of Montgomerie."

"No," replied the earl, decisively, "that name is ended. All I have to consider is my own people here—my tenants and servants. Whoever succeeds me ought to know them all, and be to them exactly what I have been, or rather what I hope to be."

"Mr. Cardross, for instance. Were you thinking of him as your heir?"

"No, not exactly," replied Lord Cairnforth, slightly coloring. "He is a little too old. Besides, he is not quite the sort of person I should wish—too gentle and self-absorbed—too little practical."

"One of his sons, perhaps?"

"No, nor one of yours either; to whom, by the way, you will please to set down a thousand pounds apiece. Nay, don't look so horrified; it will not harm them. But personally I do not know them, nor they me. And my heir should be some one whom I thoroughly do know, thoroughly respect, thoroughly love. There is but one person in the world—one young person—who answers to all these requisites."

"Who is that?"

"Helen Cardross."

Mr. Menteith was a good deal surprised. Though he had a warm corner in his heart for Helen, still, the idea of her as heiress to so large an estate was novel and '

F

startling. He did not consider himself justified in criti-
cising the earl's choice; still, he thought it odd. True,
Helen was a brave, sensible, self-dependent woman—not
a girl any longer—and accustomed from the age of fifteen
to guide a household, to be her father's right hand, and
her brothers' help and counselor—one of those rare char-
acters who, without being exactly masculine, are yet not
too feebly feminine—in whom strength is never exagger-
ated to boldness, nor gentleness deteriorated into weakness. She was firm, too; could form her own opinion
and carry it out; though not accomplished, was fairly
well educated; possessed plenty of sound practical knowledge of men and things, and, above all, had habits of extreme order and regularity. People said, sometimes, that
Miss Cardross ruled not only the Manse, but the whole
parish; however, if so, she did it in so sweet a way that
nobody ever objected to her government.

All these things Mr. Menteith ran over in his acute
mind within the next few minutes, during which he did
not commit himself to any remarks at all. At last he
said,

"I think, my lord, you are right. Helen's no bonnie,
but she is a rare creature, with the head of a man and
the heart of a woman. She is worth all her brothers put
together, and, under the circumstances, I believe you
could not do better than make her your heiress."

"I am glad you think so," was the brief answer.
Though, by the expression of the earl's face, Mr. Menteith clearly saw that, whether he had thought it or not,
the result would have been just the same. He smiled a
little to himself, but he did not dispute the matter. He

knew that one of the best qualities the earl possessed—
most blessed and useful to him, as it is to every human
being—was the power of making up his own mind, and
acting upon it with that quiet resolution which is quite
distinct from obstinacy — obstinacy, usually the last
strong-hold of cowards, and the blustering self-defense of
fools.

"There is but one objection to your plan, Lord Cairnforth. Miss Cardross is young—twenty-six, I think."

"Twenty-five and a half."

"She may not remain always Miss Cardross. She
may marry; and we can not tell what sort of man her
husband may be, or how fit to be trusted with so large a
property."

"So good a woman is not likely t℗ choose a man
unworthy of her," said Lord Cairnforth, after a pause.
"Still, could not my fortune be settled upon herself as a
life-rent, to descend intact to her heirs—that is, her children?"

"My dear lord, how you must have thought over
every thing!"

"You forget, my friend, I have nothing to do but to
sit thinking."

There was a sad intonation in the voice which affected
Mr. Menteith deeply. He made no remark, but busied
himself in drawing up the will, which Lord Cairnforth
seemed nervously anxious should be completed that very
day.

"For, suppose any thing should happen—if I died this
night, for instance! No, let what is done be done as soon
as possible, and as privately."

"You wish, then, the matter to be kept private?" asked Mr. Menteith.

"Yes."

So in the course of the next few hours the will was drawn up. It was somewhat voluminous with sundry small legacies, no one being forgotten whom the earl desired to benefit or thought needed his help; but the bulk of his fortune he left unreservedly to Helen Cardross. Malcolm and another·servant were called in as witnesses, and the earl saying to them with a cheerful smile "that he was making his will, but did not mean to die a day the sooner," signed it with that feeble, uncertain signature which yet had cost him years of pains to acquire, and never might have been acquired at all but for his own perseverance and the unwearied patience of Helen Cardross.

"She taught me to write, you know," said he to Mr. Menteith, as—the witnesses being gone—he, with a half-amused look, regarded his own autograph.

"You have used the results of her teaching well on her behalf to-day. It is no trifle—a clear income of ten thousand a year; but she will make a good use of it."

"I am sure of that. So, now, all is safe and right, and I may die as soon as God pleases."

He leaned his head back wearily, and his face was overspread by that melancholy shadow which it wore at times, showing how, at best, life was a heavy burden, as it could not but be—to him.

"Come, now," said the earl, rousing himself, "we have still a good many things to talk over, which I want to consult you about before you go," whereupon the young man opened up such a number of schemes, chiefly for the benefit of his tenantry and the neighborhood, that Mr. Menteith was quite overwhelmed.

"Why, my lord, you are the most energetic Earl of Cairnforth that ever came to the title. It would take three lifetimes, instead of a single one, even if that reached threescore and ten, to carry out all you want to do."

"Would it? Then let us hope it was not for nothing that those good folk yesterday made themselves hoarse with wishing me 'a lang life and a merry ane.' And when I die—but we'll not enter upon that subject. My dear old friend, I hope for many and many a thirtieth of June I shall make you welcome to Cairnforth. And now let us take a quiet drive together, and fetch all the Manse people up to dinner at the Castle."

Chapter the Eighth.

THE same evening the earl and his guests were sitting in the June twilight—the long, late northern twilight, which is nowhere more lovely than on the shores of Loch Beg. Malcolm had just come in with candles, as a gentle hint that it was time for his master, over whose personal welfare he was sometimes a little too solicitous, to retire, when there happened what for the time being startled every body present.

Malcolm, going to the window, sprang suddenly back with a shout and a scream.

"I kent it weel. It was sure to be! Oh, my lord, my lord!"

"What is the matter?" said Mr. Menteith, sharply. "You're gone daft, man;" for the big Highlander was trembling like a child.

"Whisht! dinna speak o't. It was my lord's wraith, ye ken. It just keekit in and slippit awa."

"Folly! I saw nothing."

"But I think I did," said Lord Cairnforth.

"Hear him! Ay, he saw 't his ain sel. Then it maun be true. Oh my dear lord!"

Poor Malcolm fell on his knees by the earl's little chair in such agitation that Mr. Cardross looked up from his book, and Helen from her peaceful needle-work, which was rarely out of her active hands.

F 2

"He thinks he has seen his master's wraith; and because the earl signed his will this morning, he is sure to die, especially as Lord Cairnforth saw the same thing himself. Will you say, my lord, what you did see?"

"Mr. Menteith, I believe I saw a man peering in at that window."

"It wasna a man—it was a speerit," moaned Malcolm. "My lord's wraith, for sure."

"I don't think so, Malcolm; for it was a tall, thin figure, that moved about lightly and airily—was come and gone in a moment. Not very like my wraith, unless the wraith of myself as I might have been."

The little party were silent till Helen said,

"What do you think it was, then?"

"Certainly a man, made of honest flesh and blood, though not much of either, for he was excessively thin and sickly-looking. He just 'keekit in,' as Malcolm says, and disappeared."

"What a very odd circumstance!" said Mr. Menteith. "Not a robber, I trust. I am much more afraid of robbers than of ghosts."

"We never rob at Cairnforth; we are very honest people here. No, I think it is far likelier to be one of those stray tourists who are brought here by the steamers. They sometimes take great liberties, wandering into the Castle grounds, and perhaps one of them thought he might as well come and stare in at my windows."

"I hope he was English; I should not like a Scotsman to do such a rude thing," cried Helen, indignantly.

Lord Cairnforth laughed at her impulsiveness. There was much of the child nature mingled in Helen's gravity and wisdom, and she sometimes did both speak and act from impulse—especially generous and kindly impulse—as hastily and unthinkingly as a child.

"Well, Malcolm, the only way to settle this difficulty is to search the house and grounds. Take a good thick stick and a lantern, and whatever you find—be it tourist or burglar, man or spirit—bring him at once to me."

And then the little group waited, laughing among themselves, but still not quite at ease. Lord Cairnforth would not allow Mr. Cardross and Helen to walk home; the carriage was ordered to be made ready.

Presently Malcolm appeared, somewhat crestfallen.

"It is a man, my lord, and no speerit. But he wadna come ben. He says he'll wait your lordship's will, and that's his name," laying a card before the earl, who looked at it and started with surprise.

"Mr. Menteith, just see—'Captain Ernest Henry Bruce.' What an odd coincidence!"

"Coincidence indeed!" repeated the lawyer, skeptically. "Let me see the card."

"Ernest Henry! was that the name of the young man whom you sent out to India?"

"How should I remember? It was ten or fifteen years ago. Very annoying! However, since he is a Bruce, or says he is, I suppose your lordship must just see him."

"Certainly," replied, in his quiet, determined tone, the Earl of Cairnforth.

Helen, who looked exceedingly surprised, offered to retire, but the earl would not hear of it.

"No, no: you are a wise woman, and an acute one too. I would like you to see and judge of this cousin of mine

—a faraway cousin, who would like well enough, Mr.
Menteith guesses, to be my heir. But we will not judge
him harshly, and especially we will not prejudge him.
His father was nothing to boast of, but this may be a
very honest man for all we know. · Sit by me, Helen,
and take a good look at him."

And, with a certain amused pleasure, the earl watched
Helen's puzzled air at being made of so much import-
ance, till the stranger appeared.

He was a man of about thirty, though at first sight he
seemed older, from his exceedingly worn and sickly appearance. His lank black hair fell about his thin, sallow
face; he wore what we now call the Byron collar and
Byron tie—for it was in the Byron era, when sentiment-
alism and misery-making were all the fashion. Certainly the poor captain looked miserable enough, without any
pretense of it; for, besides his thin and unhealthy aspect,
his attire was in the lowest depth of genteel shabbiness.
Nevertheless, he looked gentlemanly, and clever too; nor
was it an unpleasant face, though the lower half of it indicated weakness and indecision; and the eyes—large, dark,
and hollow—were a little too closely set together, a peculiarity which always gives an uncandid, and often a rather sinister expression to any face. Still, there was something about the unexpected visitor decidedly interesting.

Even Helen looked up from her work once—twice—
with no small curiosity; she saw so few strangers, and
of men, and young men, almost none, from year's end to
year's end. Yet it was a look as frank, as unconscious,
as maidenly as might have been Miranda's first glance at
Ferdinand.

Captain Bruce did not return her glance at all. His whole attention was engrossed by Lord Cairnforth.

"My lord, I am so sorry—so very sorry—if I startled you by my rudeness. The group inside was so cheering a sight, and I was a poor weary wayfarer."

"Do not apologize, Captain Bruce. I am happy to make your acquaintance."

"It has been the wish of my life, Lord Cairnforth, to make yours."

Lord Cairnforth turned upon him eyes sharp enough to make a less acute person than the captain feel that honesty, rather than flattery, was the safest tack to go upon. He took the hint.

"That is, I have wished, ever since I came home from India, to thank you and Mr. Menteith—this is Mr. Menteith, I presume?—for my cadetship, which I got through you. And though my ill health has blighted my prospects, and after some service—for I exchanged from the Company's civil into the military service—I have returned to England an invalided and disappointed man, still my gratitude is exactly the same, and I was anxious to see and thank you, as my benefactor and my cousin."

Lord Cairnforth merely bent his head in answer to this long speech, which a little perplexed him. He, like Helen, was both unused and indifferent to strangers.

But Captain Bruce seemed determined not to be made a stranger. After the brief ceremony of introduction to the little party, he sat down close to Lord Cairnforth, displacing Helen, who quietly retired, and began to unfold all his circumstances, giving as credentials of identity a medal received for some Indian battle; a letter from his

father, the colonel, whose handwriting Mr. Menteith immediately recognized, and other data, which sufficiently
proved that he really was the person he assumed to be.

"For," said he, with that exceedingly frank manner he
had, the sort of manner particularly taking with reserved
people, because it saves them so much trouble—"for
otherwise how should you know that I am not an im-
postor—a swindler—instead of your cousin, which I hope
you believe I really am, Lord Cairnforth?"

"Certainly," said the earl, smiling, and looking both
amused and interested by this little adventure, so novel
in his monotonous life.

Also, his kindly heart was touched by the sickly and
feeble aspect of the young man, by his appearance of
poverty, and by something in his air which the earl fancied implied that brave struggle against misfortune, more
pathetic than misfortune itself. With undisguised pleasure, the young host sat and watched his guest doing full
justice to the very best supper that the Castle could furnish.

"You are truly a good Samaritan," said Captain Bruce,
pouring out freely the claret which was then the universal drink of even the middle classes in Scotland. "I
had fallen among thieves (literally, for my small baggage
was stolen from me yesterday, and I have no worldly
goods beyond the clothes I stand in); you meet me, my
good cousin, with oil and wine, and set me on your own
beast, which I fear I shall have to ask you to do, for I am
not strong enough to walk any distance. How far is it
to the nearest inn?"

"About twenty miles. But we will discuss that question presently. In the mean time, eat and drink; you need it."

"Ah! yes. You have never known hunger—I hope you never may; but it is not a pleasant thing, I assure you, actually to want food."

Helen looked up sympathetically. As Captain Bruce took not the slightest notice of her, she had ample opportunity to observe him. Pity for his worn face made her lenient. Lord Cairnforth read her favorable judgment in her eyes, and it inclined him also to judge kindly of the stranger. Mr. Menteith alone, more familiar with the world, and goaded by it into that sharp suspiciousness which is the last hardening of a kindly and generous heart—Mr. Menteith held aloof for some time, till at last even he succumbed to the charm of the captain's conversation. Mr. Cardross had already fallen a willing victim, for he had latterly been deep in the subject of Warren Hastings, and to meet with any one who came direct from that wondrous land of India, then as mysterious and far-away a region as the next world, to people in England, and especially in the wilds of Scotland, was to the good minister a delight indescribable.

Captain Bruce, who had at first paid little attention to any body but his cousin, soon exercised his faculty of being "all things to all men," gave out his stores of information, bent all his varied powers to gratify Lord Cairnforth's friends, and succeeded.

The clock had struck twelve, and still the little party were gathered round the supper-table. Captain Bruce rose.

"I am ashamed to have detained you from your natu-

ral rest, Lord Cairnforth. I am but a poor sleeper myself; my cough often disturbs me much. Perhaps, as
there is no inn, one of your servants could direct me to
some cottage near, where I could get a night's lodging,
and go on my way to-morrow. Any humble place will
do; I am accustomed to rough it; besides, it suits my
finances: half-pay to a sickly invalid is hard enough—
you understand?"

"I do."

"Still, if I could only get health! I have been told
that this part of the country is very favorable to people
with delicate lungs. Perhaps I might meet with some
farm-house lodging?"

"I could not possibly allow that," said Lord Cairnforth, unable, in spite of all Mr. Menteith's grave warning
looks, to shut up his warm heart any longer. "The
Castle is your home, Captain Bruce, for as long as you
may find it pleasant to remain here."

The invitation, given so unexpectedly and cordially,
seemed to surprise, nay, to touch the young man exceedingly.

"Thank you, my cousin. You are very kind to me,
which is more than I can say of the world in general. I
will thankfully stay with you for a little. It might give
me a chance of health."

"I trust so."

Still, to make all clear between host and guest, let me
name some end to my visit. This is the first day of
July; may I accept your hospitality for a fortnight—say
till the 15th?"

"Till whenever you please," replied the earl, courteously and warmly; for he was pleased to find his cousin, even though a Bruce, so very agreeable; glad, too, that he had it in his power to do him a kindness, which, perhaps, had too long been neglected. Besides, Lord Cairnforth had few friends, and youth so longs for companionship. This was actually the first time he had had a chance of forming an intimacy with a young man of his own age, education, and position, and he caught at it with avidity, the more so because Captain Bruce seemed likely to supply all the things which he had not and never could have — knowledge of the world outside; " hairbreadth 'scapes" and adventurous experiences, told with a point and cleverness that added to their charm.

Besides, the captain was decidedly " interesting." Young ladies would have thought him so, with his pale face and pensive air, which, seeing that the Byron fever had not yet attacked the youths of Cairnforth, appeared to his simple audience a melancholy quité natural and not assumed. And his delicacy of health was a fact only too patent. There was a hectic brilliant color on his cheek, and his cough interrupted him continually. His whole appearance implied that, in any case, a long life was scarcely probable, and this alone was enough to soften any tender heart toward him.

" What does Helen think of my new cousin ?" whispered Lord Cairnforth, looking up to her with his affectionate eyes, as she bent over his chair to bid him goodnight.

" I like him," was the frank answer. " He is very agreeable, and then he looks so ill."

" Was I right in asking him to stay here ?"

"Yes, I think so. He is your nearest relation, and, as the proverb says, 'Bluid is thicker than water.'"

"Not always."

"But now you will soon be able to judge how you like him, and if you do like him, I hope you will be very kind to him."

"Do you, Helen? Then I certainly will."

The earl kept his word. Many weeks went by; the 15th of July was long past, and still Captain Bruce remained a guest at the Castle—quite domesticated, for he soon made himself as much at home as if he had dwelt there all his days. He fluctuated a little between the Castle and the Manse, but soon decided that the latter was "rather a dull house"—the boys rough—the minister too much of a student—and Miss Cardross "a very good sort of girl, but certainly no beauty," which dictum, delivered in an oracular manner, as from one well accustomed to criticise the sex, always amused the earl exceedingly.

To Lord Cairnforth, his new-found cousin devoted himself in the most cousinly way. Tender, respectful, unobtrusive, bestowing on him enough, and not too much of his society; never interfering, and yet always at hand with any assistance required: he was exactly the companion which the earl needed, and liked constantly beside him. For, of course, Malcolm, fond and faithful as he was, was only a servant; a friend, who was also a gentleman, yet who did not seem to feel or dislike the many small cares and attentions which were necessities to Lord Cairnforth, was quite a different thing. It was a touching contrast to see the two together; the active, elegant young man—for, now he was well-dressed, Captain Bruce looked remarkably elegant and gentlemanly, and the little motionless figure, as impassive and helpless almost as an image carved in stone, but yet who was undoubtedly the Earl of Cairnforth, and sole master of Cairnforth Castle.

Perhaps the wisest hit of the captain's proceedings was the tact with which he always recognized this fact, and paid his cousin that respect and deference, and that tacit acknowledgment of his rights of manhood and government which could not but be soothing and pleasant to one so afflicted. Or perhaps—let us give the kindest interpretation possible to all things—the earl's helplessness and loveableness touched a chord long silent, or never stirred before in the heart of the man of the world. Possibly—who can say?—he really began to like him.

At any rate, he seemed as if he did, and Lord Cairnforth gave back to him in double measure all that he bestowed.

As a matter of course, all the captain's pecuniary needs were at once supplied. His threadbare clothes became mysteriously changed into a wardrobe supplied with every thing that a gentleman could desire, and a rather luxurious gentleman too; which, owing to his Indian habits and his delicate health, the young captain turned out to be. At first he resisted all this kindness; but all remonstrances being soon overcome, he took his luxuries quite naturally, and evidently enjoyed them, though scarcely so much as the earl himself.

To that warm heart, which had never had half enough of ties whereon to expend itself and its wealth of gener-

osity, it was perfectly delicious to see the sick soldier
daily gaining health by riding the Cairnforth horses,
shooting over the moors, or fishing in the lochs.   Never
had the earl so keenly enjoyed his own wealth, and the
blessings it enabled him to lavish abroad; never in his
lifetime had he looked so thoroughly contented.

"Helen," he said one day, when she had come up for
an hour or two to the Castle, and then, as usual, Captain
Bruce had taken the opportunity of riding out—he owned he found Miss Cardross's company and conversation
"slow"—"Helen, that young man looks stronger and
better every day.   What a bright-looking fellow he is !
It does one good to see him."   And the earl followed
with his eyes the graceful steed and equally graceful
rider, caracoling in front of the Castle windows.

Helen said nothing.

"I think," he continued, "that the next best thing to
being happy one's self is to be able to make other people
so.   Perhaps that may be the sort of happiness they have
in the next world.   I often speculate about it, and wonder what sort of creature I shall find myself there.
But," added he, abruptly, "now to business.   You will
be my secretary this morning instead of Bruce ?"

"Willingly;" for, though she too, like Malcolm, had
been a little displaced by this charming cousin, there was
not an atom of jealousy in her nature.   Hers was that
pure and unselfish affection which could bear to stand by
and see those she loved made happy, even though it was
by another than herself.

She fell to work in her old way, and the earl employed
as much as he required her ready handwriting, her clear

head, and her full acquaintance with every body and every thing in the district; for Helen was a real minister's
daughter—as popular and as necessary in the parish as
the minister himself; and she was equally important at
the Castle, where she was consulted, as this morning, on
every thing Lord Cairnforth was about to do, and on the
wisest way of expending—he did not wish to save—the
large yearly income which he now seemed really beginning to enjoy.

Helen, too, after a long morning's work, drew her
breath with a sigh of pleasure.

"What a grand thing it is to be as rich as you are!"

"Why so?"

"One can do such a deal of good with plenty of
money."

"Yes. Should you like to be very rich, Helen?"
watching her with an amused look.

Helen shook her head and laughed. "Oh, it's no use
asking me the question, for I shall never have the chance
of being rich."

"You can not say; you might marry, for instance."

"That is not likely. Papa could never do without
me; besides, as the folk say, I'm 'no bonnie, ye ken.'
But," speaking more seriously, "indeed, I never think of
marrying. If it is to be it will be; if not, I am quite
happy as I am. And for money, can I not always come
to you whenever I want it? You supply me endlessly
for my poor people. And, as Captain Bruce was saying
to papa the other night, you are a perfect mine of gold—
and of generosity."

"Helen," Lord Cairnforth said, after he had sat think-

ing a while, "I wanted to consult you about Captain
Bruce. How do you like him? That is, do you still
continue to like him, for I know you did at first?"

"And I do still. I feel so very sorry for him."

"Only, my dear"—Lord Cairnforth sometimes called
her "my dear," and spoke to her with a tender, superior
wisdom—"one's link to one's friends ought to be a little
stronger than being sorry for them; one ought to respect
them. One must respect them before one can trust them
very much—with one's property, for instance."

"Do you mean," said straightforward Helen, "that you
have any thoughts of making Captain Bruce your heir?"

"No, certainly not; but I have grave doubts whether
I ought not to remember him in my will, only I wished
to see his health re-established first, since, had he continued as delicate as when he came, he might not even have
outlived me."

"How calmly you talk of all this," said Helen, with a
little shiver. She, full of life and health, could hardly
realize the feeling of one who stood always on the brink
of another world, and looking to that world only for real
health—real life.

"I think of it calmly, and therefore speak calmly.
But, dear Helen, I will not grieve you to-day. There is
plenty of time, and all is safe, whatever happens. I can
trust my successor to do rightly. As for my cousin, I
will try him a little longer, lest he prove

"'A little more than kin, and less than kind.'"

"There seems no likelihood of that. He always speaks
in the warmest manner of you whenever he comes to the

Manse; that is what makes me like him, I fancy; and also, because I would always believe the best of people until I found out to the contrary. Life would not be worth having if we were continually suspecting every body—believing every body bad till we had found them out to be good. If so, with many, I fear we should never find the good out at all. That is—I can't put it cleverly, like you, but I know what I mean."

Lord Cairnforth smiled. "So do I, Helen, which is quite enough for us two. We will talk this over some other time; and meanwhile"—he looked at her earnestly and spoke with meaning—"if ever you have an opportunity of being kind to Captain Bruce, remember he is my next of kin, and I wish it."

"Certainly," answered Helen. "But I am never likely to have the chance of doing any kindness to such a very fine gentleman."

Lord Cairnforth smiled to himself once more, and let the conversation end; afterward—long afterward, he recalled it, and thought with a strange comfort that then, at least, there was nothing to conceal; nothing but sincerity in the sweet, honest face—not pretty, but so perfectly candid and true—with the sun shining on the lint-white hair, and the bright blue eyes meeting his, guileless as a child's. Ay, and however they were dimmed with care and washed with tears—oceans of bitterness—that innocent, childlike look never, even when she was an old woman, quite faded out of Helen's eyes.

"Ay," Lord Cairnforth said to himself, when she had gone away, and he was left alone in that helpless solitude which, being the inevitable necessity, had grown into the

familiar habit of his life, " ay, it is all right. No harm
could come — there would be nothing neglected — even
were I to die to-morrow."

That " dying to-morrow," which might happen to any
one of us, how few really recognize it and prepare for it!
Not in the ordinary religious sense of " preparation for
death"—often a most irreligious thing—a frantic attempt
of sinning and terror-stricken humanity to strike a bal-
ance-sheet with heaven, just leaving a sufficient portion
on the credit side—but preparation in the ordinary worldly meaning—keeping one's affairs straight and clear, that
no one may be perplexed therewith afterward; forgiving
and asking forgiveness of offenses; removing evil done,
and delaying not for a day any good that it is possible
to do.

It was a strange thing; but, as after his death it was
discovered, the true secret of the wonderful calmness and
sweetness which, year by year, deepened more and more
in Lord Cairnforth's character, ripening it to a perfectness
in which those who only saw the outside of his could
hardly believe, consisted in this ever-abiding thought—
that he might die to-morrow. Existence was to him such
a mere twilight, dim, imperfect, and sad, that he never
rested in it, but lived every day, as it were, in the prospect of the eternal dawn.

Chapter the Ninth.

THIS summer, which, as it glided away, Lord Cairn-forth often declared to be the happiest of his life, ended by bringing him the first heavy affliction—external afflic-tion—which his life had ever known.

Suddenly, in the midst of the late-earned rest of a very toilsome career, died Mr. Menteith, the earl's long-faithful friend, who had been almost as good to him as a father. He felt it sorely; the more so, because, though his own frail life seemed always under the imminent shadow of death, death had never touched him before as regarded other people. He had lived, as we all unconsciously do, till the great enemy smites us, feeling as if, whatever might be the case with himself, those whom he loved could never die. This grief was something quite new to him, and it struck him hard.

The tidings came on a gloomy day in late October, the season when Cairnforth is least beautiful; for the thick woods about it make the always damp atmosphere heavy with "the moist, rich smell of the rotting leaves," and the roads lying deep in mud, and the low shore hung with constant mists, give a general impression of dreariness. The far-away hills vanish entirely for days together, and the loch itself takes a leaden hue, as if it never could be blue again. You can hardly believe that the sun will ever again shine out upon it; the white waves rise, the mountains reappear, and the whole scene grows clear and lovely, as life does sometimes if we have only patience to endure through the weary winter until spring.

But for the good man, John Menteith, his springs and winters were alike ended; he was gathered to his fathers, and his late ward mourned him bitterly.

Mr. Cardross and Helen, coming up to the Castle as soon as the news reached them, found Lord Cairnforth in a state of depression such as they had never before witnessed in him. One of the things which seemed to affect him most painfully, as small things sometimes do in the midst of deepest grief, was that he could not attend Mr. Menteith's funeral.

"Every other man," said he, sadly, "every other man can follow his dear friends and kindred to the grave, can give them respect in death as he has given them love and help during life—I can do neither. I can help no one—be of use to no one. I am a mere cumberer of the ground. It would be better if I were away."

"Hush! do not dare to say that," answered Mr. Cardross. And he sent the rest away, even Helen, and sat down beside his old pupil, not merely as a friend, but as a minister—in the deepest meaning of the word, even as it was first used of Him who "came not to be ministered unto, but to minister."

Helen's father was not a demonstrative man under ordinary circumstances; he was too much absorbed in his books, and in a sort of languid indifference to worldly matters, which had long hung over him, more or less, ever since his wife's death; but, when occasion arose, he could rise equal to it; and he was one of those comforters who knew the way through the valley of affliction by the marks which their own feet have trod.

He and the earl spent a whole hour alone together. Afterward, when sorrow, compared to which the present grief was calm and sacred, fell upon them both, they remembered this day, and were not afraid to open their wounded hearts to one another.

At last Mr. Cardross came out of the library, and told Helen that Lord Cairnforth wanted to speak to her.

"He wishes to have your opinion, as well as my own, about a journey he is projecting to Edinburg, and some business matters which he desires to arrange there. I think he would have liked to see Captain Bruce too. Where is he?"

The captain had found this atmosphere of sorrow a little too overpowering, and had disappeared for a long ride; so Miss Cardross had been sitting alone all the time.

"Your father has been persuading me, Helen," said the earl, when she came in, "that I am not quite so useless in the world as I imagined. He says he has reason to believe, from things Mr. Menteith let fall, that my dear old friend's widow is not very well provided for, and she and her children will have a hard battle even now. Mr. Cardross thinks I can help her very materially, in one way especially. You know I have made my will?"

"Yes," replied unconscious Helen, "you told me so."

"Mr. Menteith drew it up the last time he was here. How little we thought it would be really the last time! Ah! Helen, if we could only look forward!"

"It is best not," said Helen, earnestly.

"Well, my will is made. And though in it I left nothing to Mr. Menteith himself, seeing that such a return of his kindness would be very unwelcome, I insisted on doing what was equivalent—bequeathing a thousand pounds to each of his children. Was I right in that? You do not object?"

"Most assuredly not," answered Helen, though a little surprised at the question. Still, she was so long accustomed to be consulted by the earl, and to give her opinion frankly and freely on all points, that the surprise was only momentary.

"And, by the way, I mean to leave the same sum — one thousand pounds—to my cousin, Captain Bruce. Remember that, Helen ; remember it particularly, will you? in case any thing should happen before I have time to add this to my will. But to the Menteiths. Your father thinks, and I agree with him, that the money I design for them will be far better spent now, or some portion of it, in helping these fatherless children on in the world, than in keeping them waiting for my death, which may not happen for years. What do you think?"

Helen agreed heartily. It would cause a certain diminution of yearly income, but then the earl had far more than enough for his own wants, and if not spent thus, the sum would certainly have been expended by him in some other form of benevolence. She said as much.

"Possibly it might. What else should I do with it?" was Lord Cairnforth's answer. "But, in order to get at the money, and alter my will, so that in no case should this sum be paid twice over, to the injury of my heir—I must take care of my heir," and he slightly smiled, "I ought to go at once to Edinburg. Shall I?"

Helen hesitated. The earl's last journey had been so unpropitious — he had taken so long a time to recover from it — that she had earnestly hoped he would never attempt another. She expressed this as delicately as she could.

"No, I never would have attempted it for myself. Change is only pain and weariness to me. I have no wish to leave dear, familiar Cairnforth till I leave it for —the place where my good old friend is now. And sometimes, Helen, I fancy the hills of Paradise will not be very unlike the hills about our loch. You would think of me far away, when you were looking at them sometimes?"

Helen fixed her tender eyes upon him—"It is quite as likely that you may have to think of me thus, for I may go first; I am the elder of us two. But all that is in God's hands alone. About Edinburg now. When should you start?"

"At once, I think; though, with my slow traveling, I should not be in time for the funeral; and even if I were, I could not attend it without giving much trouble to other people. But, as your father has shown me, the funeral does not signify. The great matter is to be of use to Mrs. Menteith and the children in the way I explained. Have I your consent, my dear?"

For answer, Helen pointed to a few lines in a Bible which lay open on the library table: no doubt her father had been reading out of it, for it was open at that portion which seems to have plumbed the depth of all human anguish — the Book of Job. She repeated the verses:

" ' When the ear heard me, then it blessed me; and when the eye saw me, it gave witness to me;

" ' Because I delivered the poor that cried, and the fatherless, and him that had none to help him:

" ' The blessing of him that was ready to perish came upon me, and I caused the widow's heart to sing for joy.'

" That is what will be said of you one day, Lord Cairnforth. Is not this something worth living for?"

" Ay, it is!" replied the earl, deeply moved; and Helen was scarcely less so.

They discussed no more the journey to Edinburg; but Lord Cairnforth, in his decided way, gave orders immediately to prepare for it, taking with him, as usual, Malcolm and Mrs. Campbell. By the time Captain Bruce returned from his ride, the guest was startled by the news that his host meant to quit Cairnforth at daylight the next morning, which appeared to disconcert the captain exceedingly.

" I would volunteer to accompany you, cousin," said he, after expressing his extreme surprise and regret, "but the winds of Edinburg are ruin to my weak lungs, which the air here suits so well. So I must prepare to quit pleasant Cairnforth, where I have received so much kindness, and which I have grown to regard almost like home —the nearest approach to home that in my sad, wandering life I ever knew."

There was an unmistakable regret in the young man's tone which, in spite of his own trouble, went to the earl's good heart.

" "Why should you leave at all?" said he. "Why not remain here and await my return, which can not be long delayed—two months at most—even counting my slow traveling? I will give you something to do meanwhile: I will make you viceroy of Cairnforth during my absence —that is, under Miss Cardross, who alone knows all the parish affairs—and mine. Will you accept the office?"

"Under Miss Cardross?" Captain Bruce laughed, but did not seem quite to relish it. However, he expressed much gratitude at having been thought worthy of the earl's confidence.

"Don't be humble, my good cousin and friend. If I did not trust you, and like you, I should never think of asking you to stay. Mr. Cardross—Helen—what do you say to my plan?"

Both gave a cordial assent, as was indeed certain. Nothing ill was known of Captain Bruce, and nothing noticed in him unlikeable, or unworthy of liking. And even as to his family, who wrote to him constantly, and whose letters he often showed, there had appeared sufficient evidence in their favor to counterbalance much of the suspicions against them, so that the earl was glad he had leaned to the charitable side in making his cousin welcome to Cairnforth; glad, too, that he could atone by warm confidence and extra kindness for what now seemed too long a neglect of those who were really his nearest kith and kin.

Mr. Cardross also; any prejudices he had from his knowledge of the late earl's troubles with the Bruces were long ago dispersed. And Helen was too innocent herself ever to have had a prejudice at all. She said,

G 2

when appealed to pointedly by the earl, as he now often appealed to her in many things, that she thought the scheme both pleasant and advisable.

"And now, papa," added she, for her watchful eye detected Lord Cairnforth's pale face and wearied air, "let us say good-night—and good-by."

Long after, they remembered, all of them, what an exceedingly quiet and ordinary good-by it was, none having the slightest feeling that it was more than a temporary parting. The whole thing had been so sudden, and the day's events appeared quite shadowy, and as if every body would wake up to-morrow morning to find them nothing but a dream.

Besides, there was a little hurrying and confusion consequent on the earl's insisting on sending the Cardrosses home, for the dull, calm day had changed into the wildest of nights — one of those sudden equinoctial storms, that in an hour or two alter the whole aspect of things in this region.

"You must take the carriage, Helen — you and your father; it is the last thing I can do for you—and I would do every thing in the world for you if I could; but I shall, one day. Good-by. Take care of yourself, my dear."

These were the earl's farewell words to her. She was so accustomed to his goodness and kindness that she never thought much about them till long afterward, when kindness was gone, and goodness seemed the merest delusion and dream.

When his friends had departed, Lord Cairnforth sat silent and melancholy. His cousin good-naturedly tried

to rouse him into the usual contest at chess with which
they had begun to while away the long winter evenings,
and which just suited Lord Cairnforth's acute, accurate,
and introspective brain, accustomed to plan and to order,
so that he delighted in the game, and was soon as good a
player as his teacher. But now his mind was disturbed
and restless; he sat by the fireside, listening to the fierce
wind that went howling round and round the Castle, as
the wind can howl along the sometimes placid shores of
Loch Beg.

"I hope they have reached the Manse in safety. Let
me know, Malcolm, when the carriage returns. I will go
to bed then. I wish they would have remained here;
but the minister never will stay; he dislikes sleeping a
single night from under his own roof. Is he not a good
man, cousin—one of a thousand?"

"I have not the slightest doubt of it."

"And his daughter—have you in any way modified
your opinion of her, which at first was not very favorable?"

"Not as to her beauty, certainly," was the careless reply. "She's 'no bonnie,' as you say in these parts—
terribly Scotch; but she is very good. Only don't you
think good people are just a little wearisome sometimes?"

The earl smiled. He was accustomed to, and often
rather amused by his cousin's honest worldliness and outspoken skepticisms — that candid confession of badness
which always inclines a kindly heart to believe the very
best of the penitent.

"Nevertheless, though Miss Cardross may be 'no bonnie,' and too good to please your taste, I hope you will go

often to the Manse in my absence, and write me word how they are, otherwise I shall hear little—the minister's letters are too voluminous to be frequent—and Miss Cardross is not given to much correspondence."

Captain Bruce promised, and again the two young men sat silent, listening to the eerie howling of the wind. It inclined both of them to graver talk than was their habit when together.

"I wonder," said the earl, "whether this blast, according to popular superstition, is come to carry many souls away with it 'on the wings of the wind!' Where will they fly to the instant they leave the body? How free and happy they must feel!"

"What an odd fancy! and not a particularly pleasant one," replied the captain, with a shiver.

"Not unpleasant, to my mind. I like to think of these things. If I were out of the body, I should, if I could, fly back to Cairnforth."

"Pray don't imagine such dreadful things. May you live a hundred years!"

"Not quite, I hope. A hundred years—of *my* life! No. The most loving friend I have would not wish it for me." Then, suddenly, as with an impulse created by the sad events of the day—the stormy night—and the disturbed state of his own mental condition, inclining him to any sort of companionship, "Cousin, I am going to trust you, specially, in a matter of business which I wish named to the Cardrosses. I should have done so before they left to-night. May I confide to you the message?"

"Willingly. What is it about?" and the captain's

keen black eyes assumed an expression which, if the earl
had noticed, he might have repented of his trust. But
no, he never would have noticed it. His upright, honest
nature, though capable of great reserve, was utterly in-
capable of false pretenses, deceit, or self-interested diplo-
macy. And what was impossible in himself he never
suspected in other people. He thought his cousin shallow sometimes, but good-natured; a little worldly, perhaps, but always well-meaning. That Captain Bruce
could have come to Cairnforth for any other purpose than
mere curiosity, and remained there for any motive except
idleness and the pursuit of health, did not occur to Lord
Cairnforth.

"It is on the subject that you so much dislike my talking about—my own death; a probability which I have
to consider, as being rather nearer to me than it is to
most people. Should I die, will you remember that my
will lies at the office of Menteith and Ross, Edinburg?"

"So you have made your will?" said the captain,
rather eagerly; then added, "What a courageous man
you are! I never durst make mine. But then, to be
sure, I have nothing to leave—except my sword, which I
hereby make over to you, well-beloved cousin."

" Thank you, though I should have very little use for
it. And that reminds me to explain something. The
day I made my will was, by an odd chance, the day you
arrived here. Had I known you then, I should have
named you in it, leaving you—I may as well tell you the
sum—a thousand pounds, in token of cousinly regard."

"You are exceedingly kind, but I am no fortune-
hunter."

"I know that. Still, the legacy may not be useless. I shall make it legally secure as soon as I get to Edinburg. In any case you are quite safe, for I have mentioned you to my heir."

"Your heir! who do you mean?" interrupted Captain Bruce, thrown off his guard by excessive surprise.

The earl said, with a little dignity of manner, "It is scarcely needful to answer your question. The title, you are aware, will be extinct; I meant the successor to my landed property."

"Do I know the gentleman?"

"I named no gentleman."

"Not surely a lady? Not—" a light suddenly breaking in upon him, so startling that it overthrew all his self-control, and even his good breeding. "It can not possibly be Miss Helen Cardross?"

"Captain Bruce," said the earl, the angry color flashing all over his pale face, "I was simply communicating a message to you; there was no need for any farther questioning."

"I beg your pardon, Lord Cairnforth," returned the other, perceiving how great a mistake he had made. "I have no right whatever to question, or even to speculate concerning your heir, who is doubtless the fittest person you could have selected."

"Most certainly," replied the earl, in a manner which put a final stop to the conversation.

It was not resumed on any other topics; and shortly afterward, Malcolm having come in with the announcement that the carriage had returned from the Manse (at which Captain Bruce's sharp eyes were bent scrutinizingly on the earl's face, but learned nothing thence), the cousins separated.

The captain had faithfully promised to be up at dawn to see the travelers off, but an apology came from him to the effect that the morning air was too damp for his lungs, and that he had spent a sleepless night owing to his cough.

"An' nae wonder," remarked Malcolm, cynically, as he delivered the message, "for I heard him a' through the wee hours walkin' and walkin' up and doun, for a' the world like a wolf in a cage. And eh, but he's dour the day!"

"A sickly man finds it difficult not to be dour at times," said the Earl of Cairnforth.

Chapter the Tenth.

THE earl reached Edinburg in the beginning of winter, and in those days an Edinburg winter was a very gay season. That brilliant society, which has now become a matter of tradition, was then in its zenith. Those renowned supper-parties, where great wits, learned philosophers, and clever and beautiful women met together, a most enjoyable company, were going on almost every night, and drawing into their various small circles every thing that was most attractive in the larger circle outside.

Lord Cairnforth was a long time before he suffered himself to be drawn in likewise; but the business which detained him in Edinburg grew more and more tedious; he found difficulties arise on every hand, and yet he was determined not to leave until he had done all he wanted to do. Not only in money, but by personal influence, which, now that he tried to use it, he found was considerable, he furthered, in many ways, the interests of Mr. Menteith's sons. The widow, too, a gentle, helpless woman, soon discovered where to come to, on all occasions, for counsel and aid. Never had the earl led such a busy life—one more active, as far as his capabilities allowed.

Still, now and then time hung on his hands, and he felt a great lack of companionship, until, by degrees, his name and a good deal of his history got noised abroad, and he was perfectly inundated with acquaintances. Of course, he had it at his own option how much or how little he went out into the world. Every advantage that rank or fortune could give was his already; but he had another possession still—his own as much here as in the solitudes of Cairnforth, the art of making himself "weel likit." The mob of "good society," which is no better than any other mob, will run after money, position, talent, beauty, for a time; but it requires a quality higher and deeper than these, and distinct from them all, to produce lasting popularity.

This the earl had. In spite of his infirmities, he possessed the rare power of winning love, of making people love him for his own sake. At first, of course, his society was sought from mere curiosity, or even through meaner motives; but gradually, like the good clergyman with whom

"Fools who came to scoff remained to pray,"

those who visited him to stare at, or pity a fellow-creature so afflicted, remained, attached by his gentleness, his patience, his wonderful unselfishness. And some few, of noble mind, saw in him the grandest and most religious spectacle that men can look upon—a human soul which has not suffered itself to be conquered by adversity.

Very soon the earl gathered round him, besides acquaintances, a knot of real friends, affectionate and true, who, in the charm of his cultivated mind, and the simplicity of his good heart, found ample amends for every thing that nature had denied him, the loss of which he bore so cheerfully and uncomplainingly.

By-and-by, induced by these, the excellent people whom, as by mesmeric attraction, goodness soon draws to itself, he began to go out a little into society. It could be done, with some personal difficulty and pain, and some slight trouble to his friends, which last was for a long time his chief objection; for a merciful familiarity with his own affliction had been brought about by time, and by the fact that he had never known any other sort of existence, and only, as a blind person guesses at colors, could speculate upon how it must feel to move about freely, to walk and run. He had also lost much of his early shyness, and ceased to feel any actual dread of being looked at. His chief difficulty was the practical one of locomotion, and this for him was solved much easier than if he had been a man of limited means. By some expenditure of money, and by a good deal of ingenious contrivance, he managed to be taken about as easily in Edinburg as at Cairnforth; was present at church and law-court, theatre and concert-room, and at many a pleasant reunion of pleasant people every where.

For in his heart Lord Cairnforth rather liked society. To him, whose external resources were so limited, who could in truth do nothing for his own amusement but read, social enjoyments were very valuable. He took pleasure in watching the encounter of keen wits, the talk of clever conversationalists. His own talent in that line was not small, though he seldom used it in large circles; but with two or three only about him, the treasures of his well-stored mind came out often very brilliantly. Then he was so alive to all that was passing in the world outside, and took as keen an interest in politics, social ethics, and schemes of philanthropy as if he himself had been like other men, instead of being condemned (or exalted —which shall we say? *Dis aliter visum !*) to a destiny of such solemn and awful isolation.

Yet he never put forward his affliction so as to make it painful to those around him. Many, in the generation now nearly passed away, long and tenderly remembered the little figure, placed motionless in the centre of a brilliant circle—all clever men and charming women—yet of whose notice the cleverest and most charming were always proud. Not because he was an earl—nobility were plentiful enough at Edinburg then—but because he was himself. It was a pleasure just to sit beside him, and to meet his pleasantness with cheerful chat, gay banter, or affectionate earnestness.

For every body loved him. Women, of course, did; they could not help it; but men were drawn to him likewise, with the sort of reverential tenderness that they would feel toward a suffering child or woman—and something more—intense respect. His high sense of honor, his true manliness, attracted the best of all the notabilities then constituting that brilliant set; and there was not one of them worth having for a friend at all who was not, in greater or less degree, the friend of the Earl of Cairnforth.

But there was another side of his Edinburg life which did not appear till long after he had quitted Modern Athens forever—nor even then fully; not until he had passed quite away from the comments of this mortal world. Then, many a struggling author, or worn-out professional man, to whom life was all up-hill, or to whom

sudden misfortune had made the handful of "siller" a
matter of absolute salvation to both body and soul—
scores of such as these afterward recalled hours or half
hours spent in the cosy study in Charlotte Square, beside the little figure in its chair—outwardly capable of
so little, yet endowed with both the power and will to
do so much. Doing it so generously, too, and withal so
delicately, that the most sensitive went away with their
pride unwounded, and the most hardened and irreligious
were softened by it into thankfulness to One higher than
their earthly benefactor, who was only the medium
through whom the blessings came.

These were accidental offices, intermingled with the
principal dúty which the earl had undertaken, and which
he carried out with unremitting diligence—the care of
his old friend's children. He placed some at school, and
others at college; those who were already afloat in the
world he aided with money and influence—an earl's
name was so very influential, as, with an amused smile,
he occasionally discovered.

But, busy as his new life was, he never forgot his old
life and his old friends. He turned a deaf ear to all persuasions to take up his permanent abode, according as
his rank and fortune warranted, in Edinburg. He was
not unhappy there—he had plenty to do and to enjoy;
but his heart was in quiet Cairnforth. Several times,
troublesome, and even painful as the act of penmanship
was to him, he sent a few lines to the Manse. But it
happened to be a very severe winter, which made postal
communication difficult. Besides, in those days people
neither wrote nor expected letters very often. During

the three months that Lord Cairnforth remained in Edinburg he only received two epistles from Mr. Cardross,
and those were in prolix and Johnsonian style, on literary topics, and concerning the great and learned, with
whom the poor learned country minister had all his life
longed to mix, and had never been able.

Helen, who had scarcely penned a dozen letters in her
life, wrote to him once only, in reply to one of his, telling
him she was doing every thing as she thought he would
best like; that Captain Bruce had assisted her and her
father in many ways, so far as his health allowed, but he
was very delicate still, and talked of going abroad, to the
south of France probably, as soon as possible. The captain himself never wrote one single line.

At first the earl was a little surprised at this: however, it was not his habit easily to take offense at his
friends. He was quite without that morbid self-esteem
which is always imagining affronts or injuries. If people liked him, he was glad ; if they showed it, he believed
them, and rested in their affection with the simple faith
of a child. But if they seemed to neglect him, he still
was ready to conclude the slight was accidental, and he
rarely grieved over it. Mere acquaintances had not the
power to touch his heart. And this gentle heart which,
liking many, loved but few, none whom he loved ever
could really offend. He

"Grappled them to his soul with hooks of steel,"

and believed in them to the last extremity of faith that
was possible.

So, whether Captain Bruce came under the latter category or the former, his conduct was passed over, waiting for future explanation when Lord Cairnforth returned home, as now, every day, he was wearying to do.

" But I will be back again in pleasant Edinburg next winter," said he to one of his new friends, who had helped to make his stay pleasant, and was sorely regretting his departure. " And I shall bring with me some very old friends of mine, who will enjoy it as much as I shall myself."

And he planned, and even made preliminary arrangements for a house to be taken, and an establishment formed, where the minister, Helen, and, indeed, all the Cardross family, if they chose, might find a hospitable home for the ensuing winter season.

" And how they will like it!" said he, in talking it over with Malcolm one day. " How the minister will bury himself in old libraries, and Miss Cardross will admire the grand shops and the beautiful views. And how the boys will go skating on Dunsappie Loch, and golfing over Bruntsfield Links. Oh, we'll make them all so happy!" added he, with pleasure shining in those contented eyes, which drew half their light from the joy that they saw, and caused to shine in the eyes around him.

It was after many days of fatiguing travel that Lord Cairnforth reached the ferry opposite Cairnforth.

There the Castle stood, just as he had left it, its white front gleaming against the black woods, then yellow and brown with autumn, but now only black, or with a faint umber shadow running through them, preparatory to the green of spring. Between lay the beautiful loch, looking ten times more beautiful than ever to eyes which had not

H

seen it for many long months. How it danced and dim-
pled, as it had done before the squall in which the earl's
father was drowned, and as it would do many a time
again, after the fashion of these lovely, deceitful lochs,
and of many other things in this world.

"Oh, Malcolm, it's good to be at home!" said the earl,
as he gazed fondly at his white castle walls, at the ivy-
covered kirk, and the gable end of the Manse. He had
been happy in Edinburg, but it was far sweeter to come
to the dear old friends that loved him. He seemed as if
he had never before felt how dear they were, and how
indispensable to his happiness.

"You are quite sure, Malcolm, that nobody knows we
are coming? I wished to go down at once to the Manse,
and surprise them all."

"Ye'll easy do that, my lord, for there's naebody in
sight but Sandy the ferryman, wha little kens it's the
earl himsel he's keepit waiting sae lang."

"And how's a' wi' ye, Sandy?" said Lord Cairnforth,
cheerily, when the old man was rowing him across. "All
well at home—at the Castle, the Manse, and the clachan?"

"Ou ay, my lord. Except maybe the minister. He's
no weel. He's missing Miss Helen sair."

"Missing Miss Helen!" echoed the earl, turning pale.

"Ay, my lord. She gaed awa—it's just twa days sin
syne. She was sair vexed to leave Cairnforth and the
minister."

"Leave her father?"

"A man maun leave father and mither, and cleave
unto his wife — the Scripture says it. And a woman
maun just do the like for her man, ye ken. Miss Helen's

awa to France, or some sic place, wi' her husband, Captain
Bruce."

The earl was sitting in the stern of the ferry-boat alone,
no one being near him but Sandy, and Malcolm, who had
taken the second oar. To old Sandy's communication he
replied not a word—asked not a single question more—
and was lifted out at the end of the five-minutes' passage
just as usual. But the two men, though they also said
nothing, remembered the expression of his face to their
dying day.

"Take me home, Malcolm; I will go to the Manse another time. Carry me in your arms—the quickest way."

Malcolm lifted his master, and carried him, just as in
the days when the earl was a child, through the pleasant
woods of Cairnforth, up to the Castle door.

Nobody had expected them, and there was nothing
ready.

"It's no matter—no matter," feebly said the earl, and
allowed himself to be placed in an arm-chair by the fire
in the housekeeper's room. There he sat passive.

"Will I bring the minister?" whispered Malcolm, respectfully. "Maybe ye wad like to see him, my lord."

"No, no."

"His lordship's no weel pleased," said the housekeeper
to Mrs. Campbell, when the earl leant his head back, and
seemed to be sleeping. "Is it about the captain's marriage? Did he no ken?"

"Ne'er a word o't."

"That was great lack o' respect on the part o' Captain
Bruce, and he sic a pleasant young man; and Helen, too.
Miss Helen tauld me her ain sel that the earl was greatly

set upon her marriage, for the captain gaed to Edinburg just to tell him o't. And he wrote her word that his lordship wished him no to bide a single day, but to mar- ry Miss Helen and tak her awa'. She'd never hae done it, in my opinion, but for that. For the captain was at her ilka day an a' day lang, looking like a ghaist, and tellin' her he couldna live without her—and she's a ten- der heart, Miss Helen — and she was sae awfu' vexed for him, ye ken. For, sure, Malcolm, the captain did seem almost like deein'."

" Deein'!" cried Malcolm, contemptuously, and then stopped. For while they were talking the earl's eyes had opened wide, and fixed with a strange, sad, terrified look upon vacancy.

He remembered it all now — the last night he had spent at Cairnforth with his cousin — the conversation which passed between them—the questions asked, which, from his not answering, might have enabled the captain to guess at the probable disposal of his property. He could come to no other conclusion than that Captain Bruce had married Helen with the same motive which must have induced his appearance at the castle, and his eager and successful efforts to ingratiate himself there— namely, money; that the fortune which he had himself missed might accrue to him through his union with Lord Cairnforth's heiress.

How had he possibly accomplished this? How had he succeeded in making good, innocent, simple Helen love him? for that she would never have married with- out love the earl well knew. By what persuasions, en- treaties, or lies — the housekeeper's story involved some evident lies—he had attained his end, remained, and must ever remain, among the mysteries of the many mysterious marriages which take place every day.

And it was all over. She was married, and gone away. Doubtless the captain had taken his precautions to prevent any possible hinderance. That it was a safe marriage legally, even though so little was known of the bridegroom's antecedent life, seemed more than probable —certain, seeing that the chief object he would have in this marriage was its legality, to assure himself thereby of the property which should fall to Helen in the event of the earl's decease. That he loved Helen for herself, or was capable of loving her or any woman in the one noble, true way, the largest limit of charitable interpret-ation could hardly suppose possible.

Still, she had loved him — she must have done so— with that strange, sudden idealization of love which some-times seizes upon a woman who has reached—more than reached—mature womanhood, and never experienced the passion. And she had married him, and gone away with him—left, for his sake, father, brothers, friends—her one special friend, who was now nothing to her—nothing!

Whatever emotions the earl felt—and it would be al-most sacrilegious to intrude upon them, or to venture on any idle speculation concerning them—one thing was clear; in losing Helen, the light of his eyes, the delight of his life was gone.

He sat in his chair quite still, as indeed he always was, but now it was a deathlike quietness, without the least sign of that wonderful mobility of feature and cheerful-ness of voice and manner which made people so soon grow used to his infirmity — sat until his room was prepared. Then he suffered himself to be carried to his bed, which, for the first time in his life, he refused to leave for several days.

Not that he was ill—he declined any medical help, and declared that he was only "weary, weary"—at which, after his long journey, no one was surprised. He refused to see anybody, even Mr. Cardross, and would suffer no one beside him but his old nurse, Mrs. Campbell, whom he seemed to cling to as when he was a little child. For hours she sat by his bed, watching him, but scarcely speaking a word; and for hours he lay, his eyes wide open, but with that blank expression in them which Mrs. Campbell had first noticed when he sat by the housekeeper's fire.

"My bairn! my bairn!" was all she said—for she was a very simple woman—but she loved him. And, somehow, her love comforted him. "Ye maun live, ye maun live. Maybe they'll need ye yet," sobbed she, without explaining — perhaps without knowing — who "they" meant. But she knew enough of her "bairn" to know that if any thing would rouse him it was the thought of other folk.

"Do you think so, nurse? Do you think I can be of any good to any creature in this world?"

"Ay, ye can, ye can, my lord—ye'd be awfully missed gin ye were to dee."

"Then I'll no dee"—faintly smiling, and using the familiar speech of his childhood. "Call Malcolm. I'll try to rise. And, nurse, if you would have the carriage ordered — the pony carriage — I will drive down to the

Manse and see how Mr. Cardross is. He must be rather dull without his daughter."

The earl did not—and it was long before he did—call her by her name. But after that day he always spoke of her as usual to every body; and from that hour he rose from his bed, and went about his customary work in his customary manner, taking up all his duties as if he had never left them, and as if nothing had ever happened to disturb the even tenor of his life—the strange, peaceful, and yet busy life led by the solitary master of Cairnforth.

Chapter the Eleventh.

IT happened that, both this day and the day following, Mr. Cardross was absent on one of his customary house-to-house visitings in remote corners of his parish. So the earl, before meeting Helen's father, had time to hear from other sources all particulars about her marriage—at least all that were known to the little world of Cairnforth.

The minister himself had scarcely more to communicate, except the fact, of which he seemed perfectly certain, that her absence would not exceed six months, when Captain Bruce had faithfully promised to come back and live upon his half pay in the little peninsula. Otherwise Mr. Cardross was confident his "dear lassie" would never have left her father for any man alive.

It was a marriage, externally, both natural and suitable; the young couple being of equal age and circumstances, and withal tolerably well acquainted with one another, for it appeared the captain had begun daily visits to the Manse from the very day of Lord Cairnforth's departure.

"And he always spoke so warmly of you, expressed such gratitude toward you, such admiration of you—I think it was that which won Helen's heart. And when he did ask her to marry him, she would not accept him

for a good while, not till after he had seen you in Edinburg."

"Seen me in Edinburg!" repeated the earl, amazed,
and then suddenly stopped himself. It was necessary for
Helen's sake, for every body's sake, to be cautious over
every word he said; to arrive at full confirmation of his
suspicions before he put into the poor father's heart one
doubt that Helen's marriage was not as happy or as honorable as the minister evidently believed it to be.

"He told us you seemed so well," continued Mr. Cardross; "that you were in the very whirl of Edinburg society, and delighted in it; that you had said to him that
nothing could be more to your mind than this marriage,
and that if it could be carried out without waiting for
your return, which was so very uncertain, you would be
all the happier. Was not that true?"

"No," said the earl.

"You wish she had waited till your return?"

"Yes,"

The minister looked sorry; but still he evidently had
not the slightest suspicion that aught was amiss.

"You must forgive my girl," said he. "She meant no
disrespect to her dear old friend; but messages are so
easily misconstrued. And then, you see, a lover's impa-
tience must be considered. We must excuse Captain
Bruce, I think. No wonder he was eager to get our
Helen."

And the old man smiled rather sadly, and looked wist
fully round the Manse parlor, whence the familiar presence had gone, and yet seemed lingering still—in her
flower-stand, her little table, her work-basket; for Mr

Cardross would not have a single article moved. "She will like to see them all when she comes back again," said he.

"And you—were you quite satisfied with the marriage?" asked the earl, making his question and the tone of it as commonplace and cautious as he could.

"Why not? Helen loved him, and I loved Helen. Besides, my own married life was so happy; God forbid I should grudge any happiness to my children. I knew nothing but good of the lad; and you liked him too; Helen told me you had specially charged her, if ever she had an opportunity, to be kind to him."

Lord Cairnforth almost groaned.

"Captain Bruce declared you must have said it because you knew of his attachment, which he had not had courage to express before, but had rather appeared to slight her, to hide his real feelings, until he was assured of your consent."

The earl listened, utterly struck dumb. The lies were so plausible, so systematic, so ingeniously fitted together, that he could almost have deluded himself into supposing them truth. No wonder, then, that they had deluded simple Helen, and her even simpler and more unworldly father.

And now the cruel question presented itself, how far the father was to be undeceived?

The earl was, both by nature and circumstances, a reserved character; that is, he did not believe in the duty of every body to tell out every thing. Helen often argued with him, and even laughed at him, for this; but he only smiled silently, and held to his own opinion, taught by experience. He knew well that her life — her free, open, happy life, was not like his life, and never could be. She had yet to learn that bitter but salutary self-restraint, which, if it has to suffer, often for others' sake as well as for its own, prefers to suffer alone.

But Lord Cairnforth had learned this to the full. Otherwise, as he sat in the Manse parlor, listening patiently to Helen's father, and in the newness and suddenness of her loss, and the strong delusion of his own fond fancy, imagining every minute he heard her step on the stair and her voice in the hall, he must have utterly broken down.

He did not do so. He maintained his righteous concealment, his noble deceit—if that was deceit which consisted only in silence — to the very last; spending the whole evening with Mr. Cardross, and quitting him without having betrayed a word of what he dreaded — what he was almost sure of.

Though the marriage might be, and no doubt was, a perfectly legal and creditable marriage in the eye of the world, still, in the eyes of honest men, it would be deemed altogether unworthy and unfortunate, and he knew the minister would think it so. How could he tell the poor old father, who had so generously given up his only daughter for the one simple reason—sufficient reason for any righteous marriage — "Helen loved him," that his new son-in-law was proved by proof irresistible to be a deliberate liar, a selfish, scheming, mercenary knave?

So, under this heavy responsibility, Lord Cairnforth decided to do what, in minor matters, he had often noticed Helen do toward her gentle and easily-wounded fa-

ther—to lay upon him no burdens greater than he could
bear, but to bear them herself for him. And in this instance the earl's only means of so doing, for the present
at least, was by taking refuge in that last haven of wounded love and cruel suffering—silence.

The earl determined to maintain a silence unbroken as
the grave regarding all the past, and his own relations
with Captain Bruce—that is, until he saw the necessity
for doing otherwise.

One thing, however, smote his heart with a sore pang,
which, after a week or so, he could not entirely conceal
from Mr. Cardross. Had Helen left him — him, her
friend from childhood—no message, no letter? Had her
happy love so completely blotted out old ties that she
could go away without one word of farewell to him?

The minister thought not. He was sure she had written; she had said she should, the night before her marriage, and he had heard her moving about in her room,
and even sobbing, he fancied, long after the house was
gone to rest. Nay, he felt sure he had seen her on her
wedding morning give a letter to Captain Bruce, saying
"it was to be posted to Edinburg."

"Where, you know, we all believed you then were,
and would remain for some time. Otherwise I am sure
my child would have waited, that you might have been
present at her marriage. And to think you should have
come back the very next day! She will be so sorry!"

"Do you think so?" said the earl, sadly, and said no
more.

But, on his return to the Castle, he saw lying on his
study-table a letter, in the round, firm, rather boyish

hand, familiar to him as that of his faithful amanuensis of many years.

"It's surely frae Miss Helen—Mrs. Bruce that is," said Malcolm, lifting it. "But folk in love are less mindfu' than ordinar. She's directed it to Charlotte Square, Edinburg, and then carried it up to London wi' hersel', and some other body, the captain, I think, has redirected it to Cairnforth Castle."

"No remarks, Malcolm," interrupted the earl, with unwonted sharpness. "Break the seal, and lay the letter so that I can read it. Then you may go."

But, when his servant had gone, he closed his eyes in utter hopelessness of dejection, for he saw how completely Helen had been deceived.

Her letter ran thus— her poor, innocent letter—dated ever so long ago—indeed, the time when she had told her father she should write—the night before her marriage-day:

"MY DEAR FRIEND,—I am very busy, but have striven hard to find an hour in which to write to you, for I do not think people forget their friends because they have gotten other people to be mindful of too. I think a good and happy love only makes other loves feel closer and dearer. I am sure I have been greeting like a bairn, twenty times a day, ever since I knew I was to be married, whenever I called to mind you and my dear father. You will be very good to him while I am away? but I need not ask you that. Six months, he says—I mean Captain Bruce—will, according to the Edinburg doctor's advice, set up his health entirely, if he travels about in a warm climate; and, therefore, by June, your birthday, we are sure to be back in dear old Cairnforth, to live there for the rest of our days, for he declares he likes no other place half so well.

"I am right to go with him for these six months—am I not? But I need not ask; you sent me word so yourself. He had nobody to take care of him—nobody in the world but me. His sisters are gay, lively girls, he says, and he has been so long abroad that they are almost strangers. He tells me I might as well send him away to die at once, unless I went with him as his wife. So I go.

"I hope he will come home quite strong and well, and able to begin building our cottage on that wee bit of ground on the hill-side above Cairnforth which you have promised to give to him. I am inexpressibly happy about it. We shall all live so cheerily together—and meet every day—the Castle, the Manse, and the Cottage. When I think of that, and of my coming back, I am almost comforted for this sad going away—leaving my dear father, and the boys, and you.

"Papa has been so good to me, you do not know. I shall never forget it—nor will Ernest. Ernest thought he would stand in the way of our marriage, but he did not. He said I must choose for myself, as he had done when he married my dearest mother; that I had been a good girl to him, and a good daughter would make a good wife; also that a good wife would not cease to be a good daughter because she was married—especially living close at hand, as we shall always live: Ernest has promised it.

"Thus, you see, nobody I love will lose me at all, nor shall I forget them: I should hate myself if it were pos- sible. I shall be none the less a daughter to my father —none the less a friend to you. I will never, never for- get you, my dear!" (here the writing became blurred, as if large drops had fallen on the paper while she wrote.) "It is twelve o'clock, and I must bid you good-night— and God bless you ever and ever! The last time I sign my dear old name (except once) is thus to you.

"Your faithful and loving friend,

"HELEN CARDROSS."

Thus she had written, and thus he sat and read—these two, who had been and were so very dear to one another. Perhaps the good angels, who watch over human lives and human destinies, might have looked with pity upon both.

As for Helen's father, and Helen herself too, if (as some severe judges may say) they erred in suffering themselves to be thus easily deceived—in believing a man upon little more than his own testimony, and in loving him as bad men are sometimes loved, under a strong delusion, by even good women, surely the errors of unworldliness, unselfishness, and that large charity which "thinketh no evil" are not so common in this world as to be quite unpardonable. Better, tenfold, to be sinned against than sinning.

> "Better trust all, and be deceived,
> And weep that trust and that deceiving,
> Than doubt one heart which, if believed,
> Had bless'd one's life with true believing."

Lord Cairnforth did not think this at the time, but he learned to do so afterward. He learned, when time brought round its divine *amende*, neither to reproach himself so bitterly, nor to blame others; and he knew it was better to accept any sad earthly lot, any cruelty, deceit, or wrong inflicted by others, than to have been himself the evil-doer, or to have hardened his heart against any living soul by acts of causeless suspicion or deliberate injustice.

Meanwhile, the marriage was accomplished. All that Helen's fondest friend could do was to sit and watch the event of things, as the earl determined to watch—silently, but with a vigilance that never slept. Not passively neither. He took immediate steps, by means which his large fortune and now wide connection easily enabled him to employ, to find out exactly the position of Helen's husband, both his present circumstances, and, so far as was possible, his antecedents, at home or abroad. For, after the discovery of so many atrocious, deliberate lies, every fact that Captain Bruce had stated concerning himself remained open to doubt.

However, the lies were apparently that sort of falsehood which springs from a brilliant imagination, a lax conscience, and a ready tongue—prone to say whatever comes easiest and uppermost. Also, because probably following the not uncommon Jesuitical doctrine that the end justifies the means, he had, for whatever reason he best knew, determined to marry Helen Cardross, and took his own measures accordingly.

The main facts of his self-told history turned out to be correct. He was certainly the identical Ernest Henry

Bruce, only surviving son of Colonel Bruce, and had undoubtedly been in India, a captain in the Company's
service. His medals were veritable—won by creditable
bravery. No absolute moral turpitude could be discovered concerning him—only a careless, reckless life; an
utter indifference to debt; and a convenient readiness to
live upon other people's money rather than earn his own
—qualities not so rare, or so sharply judged in the world
at large, as they were likely to be by the little world of
innocent, honest Cairnforth.

And yet he was young—he had married a good wife
—he might mend. At present, plain and indisputable,
his character stood—good-natured, kindly—perhaps not
even unlovable—but destitute of the very foundations
of all that constitutes worth in a man—or woman either
—truthfulness, independence, honor, honesty. And he
was Helen's husband — Helen, the true and the good;
the poor minister's daughter, who had been brought up
to think that it was better to starve upon porridge and
salt than to owe any one a halfpenny! What sort of a
marriage could it possibly turn out to be?

To this question, which Lord Cairnforth asked himself
continually, in an agony of doubt, no answer came—no
clew whatsoever, though, from even the first week, Hel-
en's letters reached the Manse as regularly as clock-work.
But they were mere outside letters—very sweet and loving—telling her father every thing that could interest
him about foreign places, persons, and things; only of
herself and her own feelings saying almost nothing. It
was unlikely she should: the earl laid this comfort to his
soul twenty times a day. She was married now; she

could not be expected to be frank as in her girlhood; still, this total silence, so unnatural to her candid disposition, alarmed him.

But there was no resource—no help. Into that secret chamber which her own hand thus barred, no other hand could presume to break. No one could say—ought to say to a wife, "Your husband is a scoundrel."

And besides (to this hope Lord Cairnforth clung with a desperation heroic as bitter), Captain Bruce might not be an irredeemable scoundrel; and he might—there was still a chance—have married Helen not altogether from interested motives. She was so lovable that he might have loved her, or have grown to love her, even though he had slighted her at first.

"He must have loved her—he could not help it," groaned the earl, inwardly, when the minister and others stabbed him from time to time with little episodes of the courting days—the captain's devotedness to Helen, and Helen's surprised, fond delight at being so much "made of" by the first lover who had ever wooed her, and a lover whom externally any girl would have been proud of. And then the agonized cry of another faithful heart went up to heaven—"God grant he may love her; that she may be happy—anyhow—any where!"

But all this while, with the almost morbid prevision of his character, Lord Cairnforth took every precaution that Helen should be guarded, as much as was possible, in case there should befall her that terrible calamity, the worst that can happen to a woman—of being compelled to treat the husband and father, the natural protector, helper, and guide of herself and her children, as not only her own, but *their* natural enemy.

The earl did not cancel Helen's name from his will; he let every thing stand as before her marriage; but he took the most sedulous care to secure her fortune unalienably to herself and her offspring. This, because, if Captain Bruce were honest, such precaution could not affect him in the least: man and wife are one flesh—settlements were a mere form, which love would only smile at, and at which any honorable man must be rather glad of than otherwise. But if her husband were dishonorable, Helen was made safe, so far as worldly matters went—safe, except for the grief from which, alas! no human friend can protect another—a broken heart!

Was her heart broken or breaking?

The earl could not tell, nor even guess. She left them at home not a loophole whereby to form a conjecture. Her letters came regularly, from January until May, dated from all sorts of German towns, chiefly gambling towns; but the innocent dwellers at Cairnforth (save the earl) did not know this fact. They were sweet, fond letters as ever—mindful, with a pathetic minuteness, of every body and every thing at the dear old home; but not a complaint was breathed—not a murmur of regret concerning her marriage. She wrote very little of her husband; gradually, Lord Cairnforth fancied, less and less. They had not been to the south of France, as was ordered by the physicians, and intended. He preferred, she said, these German towns, where he met his own family—his father and sisters. Of these, as even the minister himself at length noticed with surprise, Helen gave no description, favorable or otherwise; indeed, did not say of her husband's kindred, beyond the bare fact that she was living with them, one single word.

Eagerly the earl scanned her letters—those long letters, which Mr. Cardross brought up immediately to the Castle, and then circulated their contents round the whole parish with the utmost glee and pride; for the whole parish was in its turn dying to hear news of "Miss Helen." Still, nothing could be discovered of her real life and feelings. And at last her friend's fever of uneasiness calmed down a little; he contented himself with still keeping a constant watch over all her movements—speaking to no one, trusting no one, except so far as he was obliged to trust the old clerk who was once sent down by Mr. Menteith, and who had now come to end his days at Cairnforth, in the position of the earl's private secretary—as faithful and fond as a dog, and as safely silent.

So wore the time away, as it wears on with all of us, through joy and sorrow, absence or presence, with cheerful fullness or aching emptiness of heart. It brought spring back, and summer—the sunshine to the hills, and the leaves, and flowers, and birds to the woods; it brought the earl's birthday—kept festively as ever by his people, who loved him better every year; but it did not bring Helen home to Cairnforth.

Chapter the Twelfth.

LIFE, when we calmly analyze it, is made up to us all alike of three simple elements—joy, sorrow, and work. Some of us get tolerably equal proportions of each of these; some unequal—or we fancy so; but, in reality, as the ancient sage says truly, "the same things come alike to all."

The Earl of Cairnforth, in his imperfect fragment of a life, had had little enough of enjoyment; but he knew how to endure better than most people. He had, however, still to learn that existence is not wholly endurance; that a complete human life must have in it not only submission, but resistance; the fighting against evil and in defense of good; the struggle with divine help to overcome evil with good; and finally the determination not to sit down tamely to misery, but to strive after happiness—lawful happiness, both for ourselves and others. In short, not only passively to accept joy or grief, but to take means to secure the one and escape the other; to "work out our own salvation" for each day, as we are told to do it for an eternity, though with the same divine limitation—humbling to all pride, and yet encouraging to ceaseless effort—"for it is GOD that worketh in us both to will and to do of His good pleasure."

That self-absorption of loss, which follows all great anguish; that shrinking up unto one's self, which is the first and most natural instinct of a creature smitten with a sorrow not unmingled with cruel wrong, is, with most high natures, only temporary. By-and-by comes the merciful touch which says to the lame, "Arise and walk;" to the sick, "Take up thy bed and go into thine house." And the whisper of peace is, almost invariably, a whisper of labor and effort: there is not only something to be suffered, but something to be done.

With the earl this state was longer in coming, because the prior collapse did not come to him at once. The excitement of perpetual expectation — the preparing for some catastrophe, which he felt sure was to follow, and the incessant labor entailed by his wide inquiries, in which he had no confidant but Mr. Mearns, the clerk, and him he trusted as little as possible, lest any suspicion or disgrace should fall upon Helen's husband—all this kept him in a state of unnatural activity and strength.

But when the need for action died away; when Helen's letters betrayed nothing; and when, though she did not return, and while expressing most bitter regret, yet gave sufficiently valid reasons for not returning in her husband's still delicate health—after June, Lord Cairnforth fell into a condition, less of physical than mental sickness, which lasted a long time, and was very painful to himself, as well as to those that loved him. He was not ill, but his usual amount of strength—so small always—became much reduced; neither was he exactly irritable—his sweet temper never could sink into irritability; but he was, as Malcolm expressed it, "dour;" difficult to please; easily fretted about trifles; inclined to take sad and cynical views of things.

This might have been increased by certain discoveries, which, during the summer, when he came to look into his affairs, Lord Cairnforth made. He found that money which he had intrusted to Captain Bruce for various purposes had been appropriated, or misappropriated, in different ways—conduct scarcely exposing the young man to legal investigation, and capable of being explained away as "carelessness"—"unpunctuality in money matters"—and so on, but conduct of which no strictly upright, honorable person would ever have been guilty. This fact accounted for another—the captain's having expressed ardent gratitude for a sum which he said the earl had given him for his journey and marriage expenses, which, though Mr. Cardross's independent spirit rather revolted from the gift, at least satisfied him about Helen's comfort during her temporary absence. And once more, for Helen's sake, the earl kept silence. But he felt as if every good and tender impulse of his nature were hardening into stone.

Hardened at the core Lord Cairnforth could never be; no man can whose heart has once admitted into its deepest sanctuary the love of One who, when all human loves fail, still whispers, "We will come in unto him, and make our abode with him"—ay, be it the forlornest bodily tabernacle in which immortal soul ever dwelt. But there came an outer crust of hardness over his nature which was years before it quite melted away. Common observers might not perceive it—Mr. Cardross even did not; still it was there.

The thing was inevitable. Right or wrong, deservedly or undeservedly, most of us have at different crises of our lives known this feeling—the bitter sense of being wronged; of having opened one's heart to the sunshine, and had it all blighted and blackened with frost; of having laid one's self down in a passion of devotedness for beloved feet to walk upon, and been trampled upon, and beaten down to the dust. And as months slipped by, and there came no Helen, this feeling, even against his will and his conscience, grew very much upon Lord Cairnforth. In time it might have changed him to a bitter, suspicious, disappointed cynic, had there not also come to him, with strong conviction, one truth—a truth preached on the shores of Galilee eighteen hundred years ago—the only truth that can save the wronged heart from breaking—that he who gives away only a cup of cold water shall in no wise lose his reward. Still, the reward is not temporal, and is rarely reward in kind. He—and He alone—to whom the debt is due, repays it; not in our, but in his own way. One only consolation remains to the sufferers from ingratitude, but that one is all-sufficing: "Inasmuch as ye have done it unto the least of these little ones, ye have done it unto Me."

All autumn, winter, and during another spring and summer, Helen's letters—most fond, regular, and (to her father) satisfactory letters—contained incessant and eager hopes of return, which were never fulfilled. And gradually she ceased to give any reason for their non-fulfillment, simply saying, with a sad brevity of silence, which one, at least, of her friends knew how to comprehend and appreciate, that her coming home at present was "impossible."

"It's very true," said the good minister, disappointed

as he was: "a man must cleave to his wife, and a woman to her husband. I suppose the captain finds himself
better in warm countries—he always said so. My bairn
will come back when she can—I know she will. And
the boys are very good—specially Duncan."

For Mr. Cardross had now, he thought, discovered
germs of ability in his youngest boy, and was concentrating all his powers in educating him for college and the
ministry. This, and his growing absorption in his books,
reconciled him more than might have been expected to
his daughter's absence; or else the inevitable necessity
of things, which, as we advance in years, becomes so
strange and consoling an influence over us, was working
slowly upon the good old minister. He did not seem
heart-broken or even heart-wounded—he did his parish
work with unfailing diligence; but as, Sunday after Sunday, he passed from the Manse garden through the kirk-
yard, where, green and moss-covered now, was the one
white stone which bore the name of "Helen Lindsay,
wife of the Reverend Alexander Cardross," he was often
seen to glance at it less sorrowfully than smilingly. Year
by year, the world and its cares were lessening and slip-
ping away from him, as they had long since slipped from
her who once shared them all. She now waited for him
in that eternal reunion which the marriage union teaches,
as perhaps none other can, to realize as a living fact and
natural necessity.

But it was different with the earl. Sometimes, in an
agony of bitterness, he caught himself blaming her—
Helen—whom her old father never blamed; wondering
how much she had found out of her husband's conduct

and character; speculating whether it was possible to touch pitch and not be defiled; and whether the wife of Captain Bruce had become in any way different from, and inferior to, innocent Helen Cardross.

Lord Cairnforth had never answered her letter—he could not, without being a complete hypocrite; and she had not written again. He did not expect it—scarcely wished it—and yet the blank was sore. More and more he withdrew from all but necessary associations, shutting himself up in the Castle for weeks together — neither reading, nor talking much to any one, but sitting quite still—he always sat quite still—by the fireside in his little chair. He felt creeping over him that deadness to external things which makes pain itself seem comparatively almost sweet. Once he was heard to say, looking wistfully at Mrs. Campbell, who had been telling him, with many tears, of a " freend o' hers" who had just died down at the clachan, " Nurse, I wish I could greet like you."

The first thing which broke up in his heart this bitter, blighting frost was, as so often happens, the sharp-edged blow of a new trouble.

He had not been at the Manse for two or three weeks, and had not even heard of the family for several days, when, looking up from his seat in church, he was startled by the apparition of an unfamiliar face in the pulpit—a voluble, flowery-tongued, foolish young assistant, evidently caught haphazard to fill the place which Mr. Cardross, during a long term of years, had never vacated, except at communion seasons. It gave his faithful friend and pupil a sensation almost of pain to see any new figure there, and not the dear old minister's, with his long white hair, his earnest manner, and his simple, short sermon. Shorter and simpler the older he grew, till he often declared he should end by preaching like the beloved apostle John, who, tradition says, in his latter days, did nothing but repeat, over and over again, to all around him, his one exhortation—he, the disciple whom Jesus loved—"Little children, love one another."

On inquiry after service, the earl found that Mr. Cardross had been ailing all week, and had had on Saturday to procure in haste this substitute. But, on going to the Manse, the earl found him much as usual, only complaining of a numbness in his arm.

"And," he said, with a composure very different from his usual nervousness about the slightest ailment, "now I remember, my mother died of paralysis. I wish Helen would come home."

"Shall she be sent for?" suggested Lord Cairnforth.

"Oh no — not the least necessity. Besides, she says she is coming."

"She has long said that."

"But now she is determined to make the strongest effort to be with us at the New Year. Read her letter—it came yesterday; a week later than usual. I should have sent it up to the Castle, for it troubled me a little, especially the postscript; can you make it out? part of it is under the seal. It is in answer to what I told her of Duncan; he was always her pet, you know. How she used to carry him about the garden, even when he grew quite a big boy! Poor Helen!"

While the minister went on talking, feebly and wan-

deringly, in a way that at another time would have struck
the earl as something new and rather alarming, Lord
Cairnforth eagerly read the letter.   It ended thus:

"Tell Dunnie I am awfully glad he is to be a minister.
I hope all my brothers will settle down in dear old Scotland, work hard, and pay their way like honest men.
And bid them, as soon as ever they can, to marry honest
women — good, loving Scotch lassies — no fremd folk.
Tell them never to fear for 'poortith cauld,' as Mr. Burns
wrote about; it's easy to bear, when it's honest poverty.
I would rather see my five brothers living on porridge
and milk—wives, and weans, and all—than see them like
these foreigners, counts, barons, and princes though they
be.   Father, I hate them all.   And I mind always the
way I was brought up, and that I was once a minister's
daughter in dear and bonnie Cairnforth."

"What can she mean by that?" said Mr. Cardross,
watching anxiously the earl's countenance as he read.

"I suppose, what Helen always means, exactly what
she says."

"That is true.   You know we used always to say
Helen could hold her tongue, though it wasn't easy to
her, the dear lassie; but she could not say what was not
the fact, nor even give the impression of it.   Therefore,
if she were unhappy, she would have told me?"

This was meant as a question, but it gained no answer.

"Surely," entreated the father, anxiously, "surely you
do not think the lassie is unhappy?"

"This is not a very happy world," said the earl, sadly.
"But I do believe that if any thing had been seriously
wrong with her Helen would have told us."

He spoke his real belief. But he did not speak of a dread far deeper, which had sometimes occurred to him, but which that sad and even bitter postscript now removed, that circumstances could change character, and that Helen Cardross and Helen Bruce were two different women.

As he went home, having arranged to come daily every forenoon to sit with the minister, and to read a little Greek with Duncan, lest the lad's studies should be interrupted, he decided that, in her father's state, which appeared to him the more serious the longer he considered it, it was right Helen should come home, and somebody, not Mr. Cardross, ought to urge it upon her. He determined to do this himself. And, lest means should be wanting—though of this he had no reason to fear, his information from all quarters having always been that the Bruce family lived more than well—luxuriously—he resolved to offer a gift with which he had not before dared to think of insulting independent Helen—money.

With difficulty and pains, not intrusting this secret to even his faithful secretary, he himself wrote a few lines, in his own feeble, shaky hand, telling her exactly how things were; suggesting her coming home, and inclosing wherewithal to do it, from "her affectionate old friend and cousin," from whom she need not hesitate to accept any thing. But though he carefully, after long consideration, signed himself her "cousin," he did not once name Captain Bruce. He could not.

This done, he waited day after day, till every chance of Helen's not having had time to reply was long over, and still no answer came. That the letter had been received was more than probable, almost certain. Every possible interpretation that common sense allowed Lord Cairnforth gave to her silence, and all failed. Then he let the question rest. To distrust her, Helen, his one pure image of perfection, was impossible. He felt it would have killed him—not his outer life, perhaps, but the life of his heart, his belief in human goodness.

So he still waited, nor judged her either as daughter or friend, but contented himself with doing her apparently neglected duty for her—making himself an elder brother to Duncan, and a son to the minister, and never missing a day without spending some hours at the Manse.

For almost the first time since her departure, Helen's regular monthly letter did not arrive, and then the earl grew seriously alarmed. In the utmost perplexity, he was resolving in his own mind what next step to take— how, and how much he ought to tell of his anxieties to her father—when all difficulties were solved in the sharpest and yet easiest way by a letter from Helen herself— a letter so unlike Helen's, so un-neat, blurred, and blotted, that at first he did not even recognize it as hers.

"*To the Right Honorable the Earl of Cairnforth:*

"My Lord,—I have only just found your letter. The money inclosed was not there. ·I conclude it had been used for our journey hither; but it is gone, and I can not come to my dearest father. My husband is very ill, and my little baby only three weeks old. Tell my father this, and send me news of him soon. Help me, for I am almost beside myself with misery!

"Yours gratefully, ·   Helen Bruce.

"—— Street, Edinburg."

Edinburg! Then she was come home!

The earl had opened and read the letter with his secretary sitting by him. Yet, dull and not prone to notice
things as the old man was, he was struck by an unusual
tone of something very like exultation in his master's
voice as he said,

" Mr. Mearns, call Malcolm to me; I must start for
Edinburg immediately."

In the interval Lord Cairnforth thought rapidly over
what was best to be done. To go at once to Helen, whatever her misery was, appeared to him beyond question.
To take Mr. Cardross in his present state, or the lad Duncan, was not desirable: some people, good as they may
be, are not the sort of people to be trusted in calamity.
And Helen's other brothers were out and away in the
world, scattered all over Scotland, earning, diligently and
hardly, their daily bread.

There was evidently not a soul to go to her help except himself. Her brief and formal letter, breaking down
into that piteous cry of " help me," seemed to come out
of the very depths of despair. It pierced to the core of
Lord Cairnforth's heart; and yet—and yet—he felt that
strange sense of exultation and delight.

Even Malcolm noticed this.

" Your lordship has gotten gude news," said he. " Is
it about Miss Helen? She's coming hame ?"

" Yes. We must start for Edinburg at once, and we'll
bring her back with us." He forgot for the moment the
sick husband, the newborn baby—every thing but Helen
herself and her being close at hand. " It's only forty-
eight hours journey to Edinburg now. We will travel

post; I am strong enough, Malcolm; set about it quickly, for it must be done."

Malcolm knew his master too well to remonstrate. In
truth, the whole household was so bewildered by this
sudden exploit — for the wheels of life moved slowly
enough ordinarily at Cairnforth—that before any body
was quite aware what had happened, the earl and his two
necessary attendants, Malcolm and Mr. Mearns—also Mrs.
Campbell—Helen might want a woman with her—were
traveling across country as fast as the only fast traveling
of that era—relays of post-horses day and night—could
carry them.

Lord Cairnforth, after much thought, left Helen's letter
behind with Duncan Cardross, charging him to break the
tidings gradually to the minister, and tell him that he
himself was then traveling to Edinburg with all the speed
that, in those days, money, and money alone, could procure. Oh, how he felt the blessing of riches! Now,
whatever her circumstances were, or might have been
once, misery, poverty, could never afflict Helen more.
He was quite determined that from the time he brought
them home, his cousin and his cousin's wife should in-
habit Cairnforth Castle; that, whether Captain Bruce's
life proved to be long or short, worthy or unworthy, he
should be borne with, and forgiven every thing—for Hel-
en's sake.

All the journey—sleeping or waking, day or night—
Lord Cairnforth arranged or dreamed over his plans, until at ten o'clock the second night he found himself driving along the familiar Princes Street, with the grim Castle rock standing dark against the moonlight; while be-

yond, on the opposite side of what was then a morass, but is now railways and gardens, rose tier upon tier, like a fairy palace, the glittering lights of the old town of Edinburg.

Chapter the Thirteenth.

THE earl reached Edinburg late at night. Mrs. Campbell entreated him to go to bed, and not seek out the street where the Bruces lived till morning.

"For I ken the place weel," said she, when she heard Lord Cairnforth inquiring for the address Helen had given. "It's ane o' thae high lands in the New Town— a grand flat wi' a fine ha' door—and then ye gang up an' up, till at the top flat ye find a bit nest like a bird's— and the folk living there are as ill off as a bird in wintertime."

The earl, weary as he had been, raised his head at this, and spoke decisively,

"Tell Malcolm to fetch a coach. I will go there tonight."

"Eh! couldna ye bide till the morn? Ye'll just kill yoursel,' my lamb," cried the affectionate woman, forgetting all her respect in her affection; but Lord Cairnforth understood it, and replied in the good old Scotch, which he always kept to warm his nurse's heart,

"Na, na, I'll no dee yet. Keep your heart content; we'll all soon be safe back at Cairnforth."

It seemed, in truth, as if an almost miraculous amount of endurance and energy had been given to that frail body for this hour of need. The earl's dark eyes were gleaming with light, and every tone of his voice was proud and manly, as the strong, manly soul, counteracting all physical infirmities, rose up for the protection of the one creature in all the world who to him had been most dear.

"You'll order apartments in the hotel, nurse. See that every thing is right and comfortable for Mrs. Bruce. I shall bring them back at once, if I can," was his last word as he drove off, alone with Malcolm: he wished to have no one with him who could possibly be done without.

It was nearly midnight when they stood at the foot of the high stair—six stories high—and Captain Bruce, they learned, was inhabiting the topmost flat. Malcolm looked at the earl uneasily.

"The top flat! Miss Helen canna be vera well aff, I doubt. Will I gang up and see, my lord?"

"No, I will go myself. Carry me, Malcolm."

And, in the old childish way, the big Highlander lifted his master up in his arms, and carried him; flight after flight, to the summit of the long dark stair. It narrowed up to a small door, very mean and shabby-looking, from the keyhole of which, when Malcolm hid his lantern, a light was seen to gleam.

"They're no awa' to their beds yet, my lord. Will I knock?"

Lord Cairnforth had no time to reply, if indeed he could have replied; for Malcolm's footsteps had been heard from within, and opening the door with an eager "Is·that you, doctor?" there stood before them, in her very own likeness, Helen Cardross.

At least a woman like enough to the former Helen to leave no doubt it was herself. But a casual acquaintance would never have recognized her.

The face, once so round and rosy, was sharp and thin; the cheek-bones stood out; the bright complexion was faded; the masses of flaxen curls—her chief beauty—were all gone; and the thin hair was drawn up close under a cap. Her dress, once the picture of neatness, was neat still, but her figure had become gaunt and coarse, and the shabby gown hung upon her in forlorn folds, as if put on carelessly by one who had neither time nor thought to give to appearances.

She was evidently sitting up watching, and alone. The rooms which her door opened to view were only two, this topmost flat having been divided in half, and each half made into just "a but and a ben," and furnished in the meanest fashion of lodgings to let.

"Is it the doctor?" she said again, shading her light and peering down the dark stair.

"Helen!"

She recognized at once the little figure in Malcolm's arms.

"You—you! And you have come to me—come your own self! Oh, thank God!"

She leant against the doorway—not for weeping; she looked like one who had wept till she could weep no more, but breathing hard in heavy breaths, like sobs.

"Set me down, Malcolm, somewhere — any where. Then go outside."

Malcolm obeyed, finding a broken arm-chair and settling his master therein. Then, as he himself afterward

told the story, though not till many years after, when
nothing he told about that dear master's concerns could
signify any more, he "gaed awa' doun and grat like a
bairn."

Lord Cairnforth sat silent, waiting till Helen had recovered herself — Helen, whom, however changed, he
would have known among a thousand. And then, with
his quick observation, he took in as much of her circumstances as was betrayed by the aspect of the room, evidently kitchen, dining-room, and bedroom in one; for at
the far end, close to the door that opened into the second
apartment, which seemed a mere closet, was one of those
concealed beds so common in Scotland, and on it lay a
figure which occasionally stirred, moaned, or coughed,
but very feebly, and for the most part lay still—very
still.

Its face, placed straight on the pillow—and as the fire
blazed up, the sharp profile being reflected in grotesque
distinctness on the wall behind—was a man's face, thin
and ghastly, the skin tightly drawn over the features, as
is seen in the last stage of consumption.

Lord Cairnforth had never beheld death—not in any
form. But he felt, by instinct, that he was looking upon
it now, or the near approach to it, in the man who lay
there, too rapidly passing into unconsciousness even to
notice his presence—Helen's husband, Captain Bruce.

The dreadful fascination of the sight drew his attention
even from Helen herself. He sat gazing at his cousin,
the man who had deceived and wronged him, and not
him only, but those dearer to him than himself—the man
whom, a day or two ago, he had altogether hated and de-

spised. He dared do neither now. A heavier hand than that of mortal justice was upon his enemy. Whatever Captain Bruce was, whatever he had been, he was now being taken away from all human judgment into the im-mediate presence of Him who is at once the Judge and the Pardoner of sinners.

Awe-struck, the earl sat and watched the young man (for he could not be thirty yet), struck down thus in the prime of his days—carried away into the other world—while he himself, with his frail, flickering taper of a life, remained. Wherefore? At length, in a whisper, he called " Helen!" and she came and knelt beside the earl's chair.

" He is fast going," said she.

" I see that."

" In an hour or two, the doctor said."

" Then I will stay, if I may ?"

" Oh yes."

Helen said it quite passively ; indeed, her whole ap-pearance as she moved about the room, and then took her seat by her husband's bedside, indicated one who makes no effort either to express or to restrain grief—who has, in truth, suffered till she can suffer no more.

The dying man was not so near death as the doctor had thought, for after a little he fell into what seemed a natural sleep. Helen leant her head against the wall and closed her eyes. But that instant was heard from the inner room a cry, the like of which Lord Cairnforth had never heard before—the sharp, waking cry of a very young infant.

In a moment Helen started up—her whole expression

changed; and when, after a short disappearance, she re-entered the room with her child, who had dropped contentedly asleep again, nestling to her bosom, she was perfectly transformed. No longer the plain, almost elderly woman; she had in her poor worn face the look—which makes any face young, nay, lovely—the mother's look. Fate had not been altogether cruel to her; it had given her a child.

"Isn't he a bonnie bairn?" she whispered, as once again she knelt down by Lord Cairnforth's chair, and brought the little face down so that he could see it and touch it. He did touch it with his feeble fingers—the small soft cheek—the first baby-cheek he had ever beheld.

"It is a bonnie bairn, as you say; God bless it!" which, as she afterward told him, was the first blessing ever breathed over the child. "What is its name?" he asked by-and-by, seeing she expected more notice taken of it.

"Alexander Cardross—after my father. My son is a born Scotsman too—an Edinburg laddie. We were coming home, as fast as we could, to Cairnforth. He"—glancing toward the bed—"he wished it."

Thus much thought for her, then, the dying man had shown. He had been unwilling to leave his wife forlorn in a strange land. He had come "as fast as he could," that her child might be born and her husband die at Cairnforth—at least so the earl supposed, nor subsequently found any reason to doubt. It was a good thing to hear then—good to remember afterward.

For hours the earl sat in the broken chair, with Helen and her baby opposite, watching and waiting for the end.

It did not come till near morning. Once during the night Captain Bruce opened his eyes and looked about him, but either his mind was confused, or—who knows?—made clearer by the approach of death, for he evinced no sign of surprise at the earl's presence in the room. He only fixed upon him a long, searching, inquiring gaze, which seemed to compel an answer.

Lord Cairnforth spoke:

"Cousin, I am come to take home with me your wife and child. Are you satisfied?"

"Yes."

"I promise you they shall never want. I will take care of them always."

There was a faint assenting movement of the dying head, and then, just as Helen went out of the room with her baby, Captain Bruce followed her with his eyes, in which the earl thought was an expression almost approaching tenderness. "Poor thing — poor thing! her long trouble is over."

These were the last words he ever said, for shortly afterward he again fell into a sleep, out of which he passed quietly and without pain into sleep eternal. They looked at him, and he was still breathing; they looked at him a few minutes after, and he was, as Mr. Cardross would have expressed it, "away"—far, far away—in His safe keeping with whom abide the souls of both the righteous and the wicked, the living and the dead.

Let Him judge him, for no one else ever did. No one ever spoke of him but as their dead *can* only be spoken of either to or by the widow and the fatherless.

* * * * * *

K

Without much difficulty — for, after her husband's death, Helen's strength suddenly collapsed, and she became perfectly passive in the earl's hands and in those of Mrs. Campbell—Lord Cairnforth learned all he required about the circumstances of the Bruce family.

They were absolutely penniless. Helen's boy had been born only a day or two after their arrival at Edinburg. Her husband's illness increased suddenly at the last, but he had not been quite incapacitated till she had gained a. little strength, so as to be able to nurse him. But how she had done it — how then and for many months past she had contrived to keep body and soul together, to endure fatigue, privation, mental anguish, and physical weakness, was, according to good Mrs. Campbell, who heard and guessed a great deal more than she chose to tell, "just wonderfu'." It could only be accounted for by Helen's natural vigor of constitution, and by that preternatural strength and courage which Nature supplies to even the saddest form of motherhood.

And now her brief term of wifehood—she had yet not been married two years — was over forever, and Helen Bruce was left a mother only. It was easy to see that she would be one of those women who remain such—mothers, and nothing but mothers, to the end of their days.

"She's ower young for me to say it o' her," observed Mrs. Campbell, in one of the long consultations that she and the earl held together concerning Helen, who was of necessity given over almost exclusively to the good woman's charge; "but ye'll see, my lord, she will look nae mair at any mortal man. She'll just spend her days in tending that wean o' hers — and a sweet bit thing it is, ye ken — by-and-by she'll get blithe and bonnie again. She'll be aye gentle and kind, and no dreary, but she'll never marry. Puir Miss Helen! she'll be ane o' thae widows that the apostle tells o' — that are 'widows indeed.'"

And Mrs. Campbell, who herself was one of the number, heaved a sigh—perhaps for Helen, perhaps for herself, and for one whose very name was now forgotten; who had gone down to the bottom of Loch Beg when the earl's father was drowned, and never afterward been seen, living or dead, by any mortal eye.

The earl gave no answer to his good nurse's gossip. He contented himself with making all arrangements for poor Helen's comfort, and taking care that she should be supplied with every luxury befitting not alone Captain Bruce's wife and Mr. Cardross's daughter, but the "cousin" of the Earl of Cairnforth. And now, whenever he spoke of her, it was invariably and punctiliously as "my cousin."

The baby too—Mrs. Campbell's truly feminine soul was exalted to infinite delight and pride at being employed by the earl to procure the most magnificent stock of baby-clothes that Edinburg could supply. No young heir to a peerage could be appareled more splendidly than was, within a few days, Helen's boy. He was the admiration of the whole hotel; and when his mother made some weak resistance, she received a gentle message to the effect that the Earl of Cairnforth begged, as a special favor, to be allowed to do exactly as he liked with his little "cousin."

And every morning, punctual to the hour, the earl had himself taken up stairs into the infantile kingdom of which Mrs. Campbell was installed once more as head nurse, where he would sit watching with an amused curiosity, that was not without its pathos, the little creature so lately come into the world—to him, unfamiliar with babies, such a wondrous mystery. Alas! a mystery which it was his lot to behold—as all the joys of life—from the outside.

But, though life's joys were forbidden him, its duties seemed to accumulate daily. There was Mr. Cardross to be kept patient by the assurance that all was well, and that presently his daughter and his grandchild would be coming home. There was Alick Cardross, now a young clerk in the office of Menteith & Ross, to be looked after, and kept from agitating his sister by any questionings; and there was a tribe of young Menteiths always needing assistance or advice—now and then something more tangible than advice. Then there were the earl's Edinburg friends, who thronged round him in hearty welcome as soon as ever they heard he was again in the good old city, and would willingly have drawn him back again into that brilliant society which he had enjoyed so much.

He enjoyed it still—a little; and during the weeks that elapsed before Helen was able to travel, or do any thing but lie still and be taken care of, he found opportunity to mingle once more among his former associates. But his heart was always in that quiet room which he only entered once a day, where the newly-made widow sat with her orphan child at her bosom, and waited for

Time, the healer, to soothe and bind up the inevitable wounds.

At last the day arrived when the earl, with his little *cortége* of two carriages, one his own, and the other containing Helen, her baby, and Mrs. Campbell, quitted Edinburg, and, traveling leisurely, neared the shores of Loch Beg.

They did not come by the ferry, Lord Cairnforth having given orders to drive round the head of the loch, as the easiest and most unobtrusive way of bringing Helen home. Much he wondered how she bore it—the sight of the familiar hills—exactly the same—for it was the same time of year, almost the very day, when she had left Cairnforth; but he could not inquire. At length, after much thought, during the last stage of the journey, he bade Malcolm ask Mrs. Bruce if she would leave her baby for a little and come into the earl's carriage, which message she obeyed at once.

These few weeks of companionship, not constant, but still sufficiently close, had brought them back very much into their old brother and sister relation, and though nothing had been distinctly said about it, Helen had accepted passively all the earl's generosity both for herself and her child. Once or twice, when he had noticed a slight hesitation of uneasiness in her manner, Lord Cairnforth had said, "I promised *him*, you remember," and this had silenced her. Besides, she was too utterly worn out and broken down to resist any kindness. She seemed to open her heart to it—Helen's proud, sensitive, independent heart—much as a plant, long dried up, withered, and trampled upon, opens itself to the sunshine and the dew.

But now her health, both of body and mind, had revived a little; and as she sat opposite to him in her grave, composed widowhood, even the disguise of the black weeds could not take away a look that returned again and again, reminding the earl of the Helen of his childhood—the bright, sweet, wholesome-natured, high-spirited Helen Cardross.

"I asked you to come to me in the carriage," said he, after they had spoken a while about ordinary things. "Before we reach home, I think we ought to have a little talk upon some few matters which we have never referred to as yet. Are you able for this?"

"Oh yes, but—I can't—I can't!" and a sudden expression of trouble and fear darkened the widow's face. "Do not ask me any questions about the past. It is all over now; it seems like a dream—as if I had never been away from Cairnforth."

"Let it be so then, Helen, my dear," replied the earl, tenderly. "Indeed, I never meant otherwise. It is far the best."

Thus, both at the time and ever after, he laid, and compelled others to lay, the seal of silence upon those two sad years, the secrets of which were buried in Captain Bruce's quiet grave in Grayfriars' church-yard.

"Helen," he continued, "I am not going to ask you a single question; I am only going to tell you a few things, which you are to tell your father at the first opportunity, so as to place you in a right position toward him, and, whatever his health may be, to relieve his mind entirely both as to you and Boy."

"Boy" the little Alexander had already begun to be

called. "Boy" *par excellence*, for even at that early period
of his existence he gave tokens of being a most masculine
character, with a resolute will of his own, and a power of
howling till he got his will which delighted Nurse Campbell exceedingly. He was already a thorough Cardross
— not in the least a Bruce: he inherited Helen's great
blue eyes, large frame, and healthy temperament, and
was, in short, that repetition of the mother in the son
which Dame Nature delights in, and out of which she
sometimes makes the finest and noblest men that the
world ever sees.

"Boy has been wide awake these two hours, noticing
every thing," said his mother, with a mother's firm conviction that this rather imaginative fact was the most interesting possible to every body. "He might have known
the loch quite well already, by the way he kept staring
at it."

"He will know it well enough by-and-by," said the
earl, smiling. "You are aware, Helen, that he and you
are permanently coming home."

"To the Manse? yes! My dear father! he will keep
us there during his lifetime. Afterward we must take
our chance, my boy and I."

"Not quite that. Are you not aware — I thought,
from circumstances, you must have guessed it long ago
—that Cairnforth Castle, and my whole property, will be
yours some time?"

Helen colored up, vividly and painfully, to the very
brow.

"I will tell you no untruth, Lord Cairnforth. I *was*
aware of it. That is, he—I mean it was suspected that

you had meant it once. I found this out—don't ask me how—shortly after I was married; and I determined, as the only chance of avoiding it—and several other things —never to write to you again; never to take the least means of bringing myself—us—back to your memory."

" Why so ?"

" I wished you to forget us, and all connected with us, and to choose some one more worthy, more suitable, to inherit your property."

" But, Helen, that choice rested with myself alone," said the earl, smiling. " Has not a man the right to do what he likes with his own ?"

" Yes; but—oh," cried Helen, earnestly, " do not talk of this. It caused me such misery once. Never let us speak of it again."

" I must speak of it," was the answer, equally earnest. " All my comfort — I will not say happiness; we have both learned, Helen, not to count too much upon happiness in this world—but all the peace of my future life, be it short or long, depends upon my having my heart's desire in this matter. It is my heart's desire, and no one shall forbid it. I will carry out my intentions, whether you agree to them or not. I will speak of them no more, if you do not wish it, but I shall certainly perform them. And I think it would be far better if we could talk matters out together, and arrange every thing plainly and openly before you go home to the Manse, if you prefer the Manse, though I could have wished it was to the Castle."

" To the Castle !"

" Yes. I intended to have brought you back from

Edinburg — *all* of you," added the earl, with emphasis, "to the Castle for life!"

Helen was much affected. She made no attempt either to resist or to reply.

"But now, my dear, you shall do exactly what you will about the home you choose — exactly what makes you most content, and your father also. Only listen to me just for five minutes, without interrupting me. I never could bear to be interrupted, you know."

Helen faintly smiled, and Lord Cairnforth, in a brief, business-like way, explained how, the day after his coming of age, he had deliberately, and upon what he — and Mr. Menteith likewise — considered just grounds, constituted her, Helen Cardross, as his sole heiress; that he had never altered his will since, and therefore she now was, and always would have been, and her children after her, rightful successors to the Castle and broad acres of Cairnforth.   •

"The title lapses," he added: "there will be no more Earls of Cairnforth. But your boy may be the founder of a new name and family, that may live and rule for generations along the shores of our loch, and perhaps keep even my poor name alive there for a little while."

Helen did not speak. Probably she too, with her clear common sense, saw the wisdom of the thing. For as, as the earl said, he had a right to choose his own heir—and as even the world would say, what better heir could he choose than his next of kin — Captain Bruce's child? What mother could resist such a prospect for her son? She sat, her tears flowing, but still with a great light in her blue eyes, as if she saw far away in the distance, far beyond all this sorrow and pain, the happy future of her darling—her only child.

"Of course, Helen, I could pass you over, and leave all direct to that young man of yours, who is, if I died intestate, my rightful heir. But I will not—at least, not yet. Perhaps, if I live to see him of age, I may think about making him take my name, as Bruce-Montgomerie. But meanwhile I shall educate him, send him to school and college, and at home he shall be put under Malcolm's care, and have ponies to ride and boats to row. In short, Helen," concluded the earl, looking earnestly in her face with that sad, fond, and yet peaceful expression he had, "I mean your boy to do all that I could not do, and to be all that I ought to have been. You are satisfied?"

"Yes—quite. I thank you. And I thank God."

A minute more, and the carriage stopped at the wicket-gate of the Manse garden.

There stood the minister, with his white locks bared, and his whole figure trembling with agitation, but still himself—stronger and better than he had been for many months.

"Papa! papa!" And Helen, his own Helen, was in his arms.

"Drive on," said Lord Cairnforth, hurriedly; "Malcolm, we will go straight to the Castle now."

And so, no one heeding him—they were too happy to notice any thing beyond themselves—the earl passed on, with a strange smile, not of this world at all, upon his quiet face, and returned to his own stately and solitary home.

Chapter the Fourteenth.

GOOD Mrs. Campbell had guessed truly that from this time forward Helen Bruce would be only a mother. Either she was one of those women in whom the maternal element predominates—who seem born to take care of other people and rarely to be taken care of themselves —or else her cruel experience of married life had forever blighted in her all wifely emotions—even wifely regrets. She was grave, sad, silent, for many months during her early term of widowhood, but she made no pretense of extravagant sorrow, and, except under the rarest and most necessary circumstances, she never even named her husband. Nothing.did she betray about him, or her personal relations with him, even to her nearest and dearest friends. He had passed away, leaving no more enduring memory than the tomb-stone which Lord Cairnforth had erected in Grayfriars' church-yard

—Except his child, of whom it was the mother's undisguised delight that, outwardly and inwardly, the little fellow appeared to be wholly a Cardross. With his relatives on the father's side, after the one formal letter which she had requested should be written to Colonel Bruce announcing Captain Bruce's death, Helen evidently wished to keep up no acquaintance whatever—nay, more than wished; she was determined it should be so—

with that quiet, resolute determination which was sometimes seen in every feature of her strong Scotch face,
once so girlish and sweet. Nor was her face unsweet
now; but it bore tokens of what she had gone through—
of a battle from which no woman ever comes out unwounded or unscarred.

But, as before said, she was a mother, and wholly a
mother, which blessed fact healed the young widow's
heart better and sooner than any thing else could have
done. Besides, in her case, there was no suspense, no
conflict of duties—all her duties were done. Had they
lasted after her child's birth the struggle might have been
too hard; for mothers have responsibilities as well as
wives, and when these conflict, as they do sometimes,
God help her who has to choose between them! But
Helen was saved this misfortune. Providence had taken
her destiny out of her own hands, and here she was, free
as Helen Cardross of old, in exactly the same position,
and going through the same simple round of daily cares
and daily avocations which she had done as the minister's active and helpful daughter.

For as nothing else but the minister's daughter would
she, for the present, be recognized at Cairnforth. Lord
Cairnforth's intentions toward herself or her son she insisted on keeping wholly secret, except, of course, as regarded that dear and good father.

"I may die," she said to the earl—"die before yourself; and if my boy grows up, you may not love him, or
he may not deserve your love, in which case you must
choose another heir. No, you shall be bound in no way
externally; let all go on as heretofore. I will have it so."

And of all Lord Cairnforth's generosity she would accept of nothing for herself except a small annual sum,
which, with her widow's pension from the East India
Company, sufficed to make her independent of her father; but she did not refuse kindness to her boy.

Never was there such a boy. "Boy" he was called
from the first, never "baby;" there was nothing of the
baby about him. Before he was a year old he ruled his
mother, grandfather, and Uncle Duncan with a rod of
iron. Nay, the whole village were his slaves. "Miss
Helen's bairn" was a little king every where. It might
have gone rather hard for the poor wee fellow thus alle-
gorically

> "Wearing on his baby brow the round
> And top of sovereignty"—

that dangerous sovereignty for any child—any human
being—to wield, had there not been at least one person
who was able to assume authority over him.

This was, strange to say—and yet not strange—the
Earl of Cairnforth.

From his earliest babyhood Boy had been accustomed
to the sight of the motionless figure in the moving chair,
who never touched him, but always spoke so kindly and
looked round so smilingly; whom, he could perceive—
for children are quicker to notice things than we sometimes think—his mother and grandfather invariably welcomed with such exceeding pleasure, and treated with
never-failing respect and tenderness. And, as soon as he
could crawl, the footboard of the mysterious wheeled
chair became to the little man a perfect treasure-house
of delight. Hidden there he found toys, picture-books,

"sweeties"—gifts such as he got nowhere else, and for which, before appropriating them, he was carefully taught to express thanks in his own infantile way, and made to understand fully from whom they came.

"It's bribery, and against my principles," the earl would sometimes say, half sadly. "But, if I did not give him things, how else could Boy learn to love me?"

Helen never answered this, no more than she used to answer many similar speeches in the earl's childhood. She knew time would prove them all to be wrong.

What sort of idea the child really had of this wonderful donor, the source of most of his pleasures, who yet was so different externally from every body else; who never moved from the wheel-chair; who neither caressed him nor played with him, and whom he was not allowed to play with, but only lifted up sometimes to kiss softly the kind face which always smiled down upon him with a sort of "superior love"—what the child's childish notion of his friend was no one could of course discover. But it must have been a mingling of awe and affectionateness; for he would often—even before he could walk—crawl up to the little chair, steady himself by it, and then look into Lord Cairnforth's face with those mysterious baby eyes, full of questioning, but yet without the slightest fear. And once, when his mother was teaching him his first hymn—

"Gentle Jesus, meek and mild,
　Look upon a little child,"

Boy startled her by the sudden remark—one of the divine profanities that are often falling from the innocent lips of little children—

"I know Jesus. He is the earl."

And then Helen tried, in some simple way, to make the child understand about Lord Cairnforth, and how he had been all his life so heavily afflicted; but Boy could not comprehend it as affliction at all. There seemed to him something not inferior, but superior to all other people in that motionless figure, with its calm sweet face—who was never troubled, never displeased—whom everybody delighted to obey, and at whose feet lay treasures untold.

"I think Boy likes me," Lord Cairnforth would say, when he met the upturned beaming face as the child, in an ecstasy of expectation, ran to meet him. "His love may last as long as the playthings do."

But the earl was mistaken, as Helen knew. His love-victory had been in something deeper than toys and "goodies." Even when their charm began to cease Boy still crept up to the little chair, and looked from the empty footboard up to the loving face, which no one, man, woman, or child, ever regarded without something far higher than pity.

And, by degrees, Boy, or "Carr"—which, as being the diminutive for his second Christian name, Cardross, he was often called now—found a new attraction in his friend. He would listen with wide-open eyes, and attention that never flagged, to the interminable "'tories" which the earl told him, out of the same brilliant imagination which had once used to delight his uncles in the boat. And so, little by little, the child and the man grew to be "a pair of friends"—familiar and fond, but with a certain tender reverence always between them, which had the most salutary effect on the younger.

Whenever he was sick, or sorry, or naughty — and Master "Boy" could be exceedingly naughty sometimes —the voice which had most influence over him, the influence to which he always succumbed, came from the little wheeled chair. No anger did he ever find there— no dark looks or sharp tones—but he found steady, unbending authority; the firm will which never passed over a single fault, or yielded to a single whim. In his wildest passions of grief or wrath, it was only necessary to say to the child, "If the earl could see you!" to make him pause; and many and many a time, whenever motherly authority, which in this case was weakened both by occasional over-indulgence and by an almost morbid terror of the results of the same, failed to conquer the child, Helen used, as a last resource, to bring him in her arms, set him down beside Lord Cairnforth, and leave him there. She never came back but she found Boy "good."

"He makes me good, too, I think," the earl would say now and then, "for he makes me happy."

It was true. Lord Cairnforth never looked otherwise than happy when he had beside him that little blossom of hope of the new generation—Helen's child.

As years went by, though he still lived alone at the Castle, it was by no means the secluded life of his youth and early manhood. He gradually gathered about him neighbors and friends. He filled his house occasionally with guests, of his own rank and of all ranks; people notable and worthy to be known. He became a "patron," as they called it in those days, of art and literature, and assembled around him all who, for his pleasure and their own benefit, chose to enjoy his hospitality.

In a quiet way, for he .disliked public show, he was likewise what was termed a "philanthropist," but always on the system which he had learned in his boyhood from Helen and Mr. Cardross, that "charity begins at home;" with the father who guides well his own household; the minister whose footstep is welcomed at every door in his own parish; the proprietor whose just, wise, and merciful rule make him sovereign absolute in his own estate. This last especially was the character given along all the country-side to the Earl of Cairnforth.

His was not a sad existence; far from it. None who knew him, and certainly none who ever staid long with him in his own home, went away with that impression. He enjoyed what he called "a sunshiny life"—having sunshiny faces about him; people who knew how to accept the sweet and endure the bitter; to see the heavenly side even of sorrow; to do good to all, and receive good from all; avoiding all envies, jealousies, angers, and strifes, and following out literally the apostolic command, "As much as in you lies, live peaceably with all men."

And so the earl was, in the best sense of the .word, popular. Every body liked him, and he liked every body. But deep in his heart—ay, deeper than any of these his friends and acquaintance ever dreamed—steadying and strengthening it, keeping it warm for all human uses, yet calm with the quiet sadness of an eternal want, lay all those emotions which are not likings, but loves; not sympathies, but passions; but which with him were to be, in this world, forever dormant and unfulfilled.

Never, let the Castle be ever so full of visitors, or let his daily cares, his outward interests, and his innumera-

ble private charities be ever so great, did he omit driving
over twice or thrice a week to spend an hour or two at
the Manse—in winter, by the study fire; in summer, under
the shade of the green elm-trees—the same trees where
he had passed that first sunny Sunday when he came a
poor, lonely, crippled orphan child into the midst of the
large, merry family—all scattered now.

The minister, Helen, and Boy were the sole inmates
left at the Manse, and of these three the latter certainly
was the most important. Hide it as she would, the principal object of the mother's life was her only child.
Many a time, as Lord Cairnforth sat talking with her,
after his old fashion, of all his interests, schemes, labors,
and hopes—hopes solely for others, and labors, the end
of which he knew he would never see—he would smile
to himself, noticing how Helen's eye wandered all the
while—wandered to where that rosy young scapegrace
rode his tiny pony—the earl's gift—up and down the
gravel walks, or played at romps with Malcolm, or dug
holes in the flower-beds, or got into all and sundry of the
countless disgraces which were forever befalling Boy;
yet which, so lovable was the little fellow, were as continually forgiven, and, behind his back, even exalted into
something very like merits.

But once—and it was an incident which, whether or
not Mrs. Bruce forgot it herself, her friend never did,
since it furnished a key to much of the past, and a serious
outlook for the future—Boy committed an error which
threw his mother into an agony of agitation such as she
had not betrayed since she came back, a widow, to Cairnforth.

Her little son told a lie! It was a very small lie, such as dozens of children tell—are punished and pardoned—but a lie it was. It happened one August morning, when the raspberries were ripe—those huge red and white raspberries for which the Manse was famous. He was desired not to touch them—" not to lay a finger on them," insisted the mother. And he promised. But, alas! the promises of four years old are not absolutely reliable; and so that which happened once in a more ancient garden happened in the garden of the Manse. Boy plucked and ate. He came back to his mother with his white pinafore all marked, and his red mouth redder still with condemnatory stains. Yet, when asked " if he had touched the raspberries," he opened that wicked mouth and said, unblushingly, " No!"

Of course it was an untruth—self-evident; in its very simplicity almost amusing; but the earl was not prepared for the effect it seemed to have upon Helen. She started back, her lips actually blanched and her eyes glowing.

" My son has told a lie!" she cried, and kept repeating it over and over again. " My son has looked me in the face and told me a lie—his first lie!"

" Hush, Helen!" for her manner seemed actually to frighten the child.

" No, I can not pass it over! I dare not! He must be punished. Come!"

She seized Boy by the hand, looking another way, and was moving off with him, as if she hardly knew what she was doing.

" Helen!" called the earl, almost reproachfully; for, in his opinion, out of all comparison with the offense seemed the bitterness with which the mother felt it, and was about to punish it. " Tell me, first, what are you going to do with the child ?"

" I hardly know—I must think—must pray. What if my son, my only son, should inherit—I mean, if he should grow up to be a liar?"

That word " inherit" betrayed her. No wonder now at the mother's agony of fear—she who was mother to Captain Bruce's son. Lord Cairnforth guessed it all.

" I understand," said he. " But—"

" No," Helen interrupted, " you need understand noth-ing, for I have told you nothing. Only I must kill the sin—the fatal sin—at the very root. I *must* punish him. Come, child !"

She was trembling all over with agitation.

" Come back, Helen," said the earl; and something in the tone made her obey at once, as occasionally during her life Helen had been glad to obey him, and creep un-der the shelter of a stronger will and clearer judgment than her own. " You are altogether mistaken, my dear friend. Your boy is only a child, and errs as such, and you treat him as if he had sinned like a grown-up man. Be reasonable. We will both take care of him. No fear that he will turn out a liar !"

Helen hesitated; but still her looks were so angry and stern, all the mother vanished out of them, that the boy, instead of clinging to her, ran away crying, and hid him-self behind Lord Cairnforth's chair.

" Leave him to me, Helen. Can not you trust me— *me*—with your son ?"

Mrs. Bruce paused.

"Now," said the earl, wheeling himself round a little, so that he came face to face with the sobbing child, "lift up your head, Boy, and speak the truth like a man to me and to your mother—see! she is listening. Did you touch those raspberries?"

"No!"

"Cardross!" calling him by his rarely-spoken name, not his pet-name, and fixing upon him eyes, not angry, but clear and searching, that compelled the truth even from a child, "think again. You *must* tell us!"

"No, me didn't touch them," answered Boy, dropping his head in conscious shame. "Not with me fingers. Me just opened me mouth and they popped in."

Lord Cairnforth could hardly help smiling at the poor little sinner—the infant Jesuit attaining his object by such an ingenious device; but the mother did not smile, and her look was harder than ever.

"You hear! If not a lie, it was a prevarication. He who lies is a scoundrel, but he who prevaricates is a scoundrel and coward too. Sooner than Boy should grow up like—like that, I would rather die. No, I would rather see him die; for I might come in time to hate my own son."

By these fierce words, and by the gleaming eyes, which made a sudden and total change in the subdued manner, and the plain, almost elderly face under the widow's cap that Helen always wore, Lord Cairnforth guessed, more than he had ever guessed before, of what the sufferings of her married life had been.

"My friend," he said, and there was infinite pity as well as tenderness in his voice, "believe me, you are

wrong.   You are foreboding what, please God, will never happen.   God does not deal with us in that manner.
He bids us do His will, each of us individually, without
reference to the doings or misdoings of any other person.
And if we obey Him, I believe He takes care we shall
not suffer—at least not forever, even in this world.   Do
not be afraid.   Boy," calling the little fellow, who was
now sobbing in bitterest contrition behind the wheeled
chair, "come and kiss your mother.   Promise her that
you will never again vex her by telling a lie."

"No, no, no.   Me'll not vex mamma.   Good mamma!
pretty mamma!   Boy so sorry!"

And he clung closely and passionately to his mother,
kissing her averted face twenty times over.

"You see, Helen, you need not fear," said the earl.

Helen burst into tears.

After that day it came to be a general rule that, when
she could not manage him herself, which not unfrequent-
ly happened — for the very similarity in temperament
and disposition between the mother and son made their
conflicts, even at this early age, longer and harder —
Helen brought Boy up to the Castle and left him, sometimes for hours together, in the library with Lord Cairnforth.   He always came home to the Manse quiet and
"good."

And so out of babyhood into boyhood, and thence
into youth, grew the earl's adopted son; for practically
it became that relationship, though no distinct explanation was ever given, or any absolute information vouch-
safed, for indeed there was none who had a right to inquire; still, the neighborhood and the public at large

took it for granted that such were Lord Cairnforth's intentions toward his little cousin.

As for the boy's mother, she led a life very retired—more retired than even Helen Cardross, doing all her duties as the minister's daughter, but seldom appearing in society. And society speculated little about her. Sometimes, when the Castle was full of guests, Mrs. Bruce appeared among them, still in her widow's weeds, to be received by Lord Cairnforth with marked attention and respect—always called "my cousin," and, whoever was present, invariably requested to take the head of his table; but, except at these occasional seasons, and at birthdays, new years, and so on, Helen was seldom seen out of the Manse, and was very little known to the earl's ordinary acquaintance.

But every body in the whole peninsula knew the minister's grandson, young Master Bruce. The boy was tall of his age — not exactly handsome, being too like his mother for that; nevertheless, the robustness of form, which in her was too large for comeliness, became in him only manly size and strength. He was athletic, graceful, and active; he learned to ride almost as soon as he could walk; and, under Malcolm's charge, was early initiated in all the mysteries of moor and loch. By fourteen years of age Cardross Bruce was the best shot, the best fisher, the best hand at an oar, of all the young lads in the neighborhood.

Then, too, though allowed to run rather wild, he was unmistakably a gentleman. Though he mixed freely with every body in the parish, he was neither haughty nor over-familiar with any one. He had something of

L

the minister's manner with inferiors—frank, gentle, and free—winning both trust and love, and yet it was impossible to take liberties with him. And some of the elder people in the clachan declared the lad had at times just "the merry glint o' the minister's e'en" when Mr. Cardross first came to the parish as a young man with his young wife.

He was an old man now, "wearin' awa'," but slowly and peacefully; preaching still, though less regularly; for, to his great delight, his son Duncan, having come out creditably at college, had been appointed his assistant and successor. Uncle Duncan—only twelve years his nephew's senior—was also appointed by Lord Cairnforth tutor to "Boy" Bruce. The two were very good friends, and not unlike one another. "Ay, he's just a Cardross," was the universal remark concerning young Bruce. No one ever hinted that the lad was like his father.

He was not. Nature seemed mercifully to have forgotten to perpetuate that type of character which had given Mr. Menteith formerly, and others since, such a justifiable dread of the Bruce family, and such a righteous determination to escape them. Not to injure them —only to escape them. Lord Cairnforth still paid the annuity, but on condition that no one of his father's kindred should ever interfere, in the smallest degree, with Helen's child.

This done, both he and she trusted to the strong safeguards of habit and education, and all other influences which so strongly modify character, to make the boy all that they desired him to be, and to counteract those tendencies which, as Lord Cairnforth plainly perceived, were

Helen's daily dread. It was a struggle, mysterious as that which visible human free-will is forever opposing (apparently) to invisible fate, the end of which it is impossible to see, and yet we struggle on.

Thus laboring together with one hope, one aim, and one affection, all centred in this boy, Lord Cairnforth and Mrs. Bruce passed many a placid year. And when the mother's courage failed her—when her heart shrank in apprehension from real terrors or from chimeras of her own creating, her friend taught her to fold patiently her trembling hands, and say, as she herself and the minister had first taught him in his forlorn boyhood, the one only prayer which calms fear and comforts sorrow—the lesson of the earl's whole life—"Thy will be done!"

Chapter the Fifteenth.

"HELEN, that boy of yours ought to be sent to col-
ge."

"Oh no! Surely you do not think it necessary ?" said
elen, visibly shrinking.

She and Lord Cairnforth were sitting together in the
ıstle library. Young Cardross had been sitting beside
em, holding a long argument with his mother, as he
ten did, for he was of a decidedly argumentative turn
mind, until, getting the worst of the battle, and being
ther "put down"—a position rarely agreeable to the
lf-esteem of eighteen—he had flushed up angrily, made
, reply, but opened one of the low windows and leaped
t on-the terrace. There, pacing to and fro along the
untess's garden, they saw the boy, or rather young
ın, for he looked like one now. He moved with a
pid step, the wind tossing his fair curls—Helen's curls
er again—and cooling his cheeks as he tried to recover
; temper, which he did not often lose, especially in the
rl's presence.

Experience had not effaced the first mysterious im-
ession made on the little child's mind by the wheeled
air and its occupant. If there was one person in the
ırld who had power to guide and control this high-
irited lad, it was Lord Cairnforth. And as the latter
ıved his chair a little round, so that he could more

easily look out into the garden and see the graceful figure sauntering among the flower-beds, it was evident by
his expression that the earl loved Helen's boy very
dearly.

"He is a fine fellow, and a good fellow as ever was
born, that young man of yours. Still, as I have told you
many a time, he would be all the better if he were sent
to college."

"For his education? I thought Duncan was fully
competent to complete that."

"Not altogether. But, for many reasons, I think it
would be advisable for him to go from home for a while."

"Why? Because his mother spoils him?"

The earl smiled, and gave no direct answer. In truth,
the harm Helen did her boy was not so much in her
"spoiling"—love rarely injures—as in the counteracting
weight which she sometimes threw on the other side—in
the sudden tight rein which she drew upon his little fol-
lies and faults—the painful clashing of two equally
strong wills, which sometimes happened between the
mother and son.

This was almost inevitable, with Helen's peculiar character. As she sat there, the sun shining on her fair face
—still fair; a clear, healthy red and white, though she
was over forty—you might trace some harsh lines in it,
and see clearly that, save for her exceeding unselfishness
and lovingness of disposition, Mrs. Bruce might in middle age have grown into what is termed a "hard" woman; capable of passionate affection, but of equally passionate severity, and prone to exercise both alike upon
the beings most precious to her on earth.

"I fear it is not a pleasant doctrine to preach to mothers," said Lord Cairnforth; "but, Helen, all boys ought to leave home some time. How else are they to know the world?"

"I do not wish my boy to know the world."

"But he must. He ought. Remember his life is likely to be a very different one from either yours or mine."

"Do not let us think of that," said Helen, uneasily.

"My friend, I have been thinking of it ever since he was born—or, at least, ever since he came to Cairnforth. That day seems almost like yesterday, and yet—We are growing quite middle-aged folk, Helen, my dear."

Helen sighed. These peaceful, uneventful years, how fast they had slipped by! She began to count them after the only fashion by which she cared to count any thing now. "Yes, Cardross will be a man—actually and legally a man—in little more than two years."

"That is just what I was considering. By that time we must come to some decision on a subject which you will never let me speak of; but by-and-by, Helen, you must. Do you suppose that your son guesses, or that any body has ever told him, what his future position is to be?"

"I think not. There was nobody to tell him, for nobody knew. No," continued Helen, speaking strongly and decidedly, "I am determined on one point—nothing shall bind you as regards my son er me—nothing, except your own free will. To talk of me as your successor is idle. I am older than you are; and you must not be compromised as regards my son. He is a good boy now, but temptation is strong, and," with an irrepressible shud-

L 2

der, "appearances are deceitful sometimes. Wait, as I
have always said—wait till you see what sort of man
Cardross turns out to be."

Lord Cairnforth made no reply, and once more the two
friends sat watching the unconscious youth, who had been
for so many years the one object of both their lives.

"Ignorance is not innocence," said the earl at length,
after a long fit of musing. "If you bind a creature mor-
ally hand and foot, how can it ever learn to walk? It
would, as soon as you loosed the bonds, find itself not
free, but paralyzed—as helpless a creature as myself."

Helen turned away from watching her boy, and laid
her hand tenderly, in her customary caress, on the feeble
hand, which yet had been the means of accomplishing so
much.

"You should not speak so," she said. "Scarcely ever
is there a more useful life than yours."

"More useful, certainly, than any one once expected
—except you, Helen. I have tried to make you not
ashamed of me these thirty years."

"Is it so many? Thirty years since the day you first
came to the Manse?"

"Yes; you know I was forty last birthday. Who
would have thought my life would have lasted so long?
But it can not last forever; and before I am 'away,' as
your dear old father would say, I should like to leave
you quite settled and happy about that boy."

"Who says I am not happy?" answered Mrs. Bruce,
rather sharply.

"Nobody; but I see it myself sometimes—when you
get that restless, anxious look—there it is now! Helen,

I must have it away. I think it would trouble me in my grave if I left you unhappy," added the earl, regarding her with that expression of yearning tenderness which she had been so used to all her days that she rarely noticed it until the days came when she saw it no more.

"I am not unhappy," she said, earnestly. "Why should I be? My dear father keeps well still — he enjoys a green old age. And is not my son growing up every thing that a mother's heart could desire?"

"I do believe it. Cardross is a good boy — a very good boy. But the metal has never been tested—as the soundest metal always requires to be — and until this is done, you will never rest. I had rather it were done during my lifetime than afterward. Helen, I particular-ly wish the boy to go to college."

The earl spoke so decidedly that Mrs. Bruce replied with only the brief question "Where?"

"To Edinburg; because there he would not be left quite alone. His uncle Alick would keep an eye upon him, and he could be boarded with Mrs. Menteith, whose income would be none the worse for the addition I would make to it; for of course, Helen, if he goes, it must be — not exactly as my declared heir, since you dislike that so much, but — as my cousin and nearest of kin, which he is undeniably."

Helen acquiesced in silence.

"I have a right to him, you see," said Lord Cairnforth, smiling, "and really I am rather proud of my young fel-low. He may not be very clever—the minister says he is not — but he is what I call a man. Like his mother, who never was clever, but yet was every inch a woman

—the best woman, in all relations of life, that I ever knew."

Helen smiled too—a little sadly, perhaps—but soon her mind recurred from all other things to her one promi-nent thought.

"And what would you do with the boy himself? He knows nothing of money—has never had a pound-note in his pocket all his life."

"Then it is high time he should have—and a good many of them. I shall pay Mrs. Menteith well for his board, but I shall make him a sufficient allowance be-sides. He must learn how to manage his money—and himself. He must stand on his own feet, without any one to support him. It is the only way to make a boy into a man—a man that is worth any thing. Do you not see that yourself?"

"I see, Lord Cairnforth, that you think it would be best for my boy to be separated from his mother."

She spoke in a hurt tone, and yet with a painful con-sciousness that what she said was not far off the truth, more especially as the earl did not absolutely deny the accusation.

"I think, my dear Helen, that it would be better if he were separated from us all for a time. We are such quiet, old-fashioned folks at Cairnforth, he may come to weary of us, you know. But my strongest motive is ex-actly what I stated—that he should be left to himself, to feel his own strength and the strength of those principles which we have tried to give him—that any special char-acter he possesses may have free space to develop itself. Up to a certain point we can take care of our children;

beyond, we can not—nay, we ought not; they must take care of themselves. I believe—do not be angry, Helen —but I believe there comes a time in every boy's life when the wisest thing even his mother can do for him is —to leave him alone."

"And not watch over him—not guide him?"

"Yes, but not so as to vex him by the watching and the guiding. However, we will talk of this another day. Here the lad comes."

And the earl's eyes brightened almost as much as Helen's did when Cardross leaped in at the window, all his good-humor restored, kissed his mother in his rough, fond way, of which he was not in the least ashamed as yet, and sat down by the wheeled chair with that tender respectfulness and involuntary softening of manner and tone which he never failed to show toward Lord Cairnforth, and had never shown so much to any other human being.

Ay, the earl had his compensations. We all have, if we know it.

Gradually, in many a long, quiet talk, during which she listened to his reasonings as probably she would have listened to no other man's, he contrived to reconcile Mrs. Bruce to the idea of parting with her boy—their first separation, even for a day, since Cardross was born. It was neither for very long nor very far, since civilization had now brought Edinburg to within a few hours' journey of Cairnforth; but it was very sore, nevertheless, to both mother and son.

Helen took her boy and confided him to Mrs. Menteith herself; but she could not be absent for more than one day, for just about this time her father's "green old age" began to fail a little, and he grew extremely dependent upon her, which, perhaps, was the best thing that could have happened to her at this crisis. She had to assume that tenderest, happiest duty of being "nursing mother" to the second childhood of one who throughout her own childhood, youth, and middle age had been to her every thing that was honored and deserving honor—loving, and worthy of love—in a parent.

Not that Mr. Cardross had sank into any helpless state of mind or body; the dread of paralysis had proved a false alarm; and Helen's coming home, to remain there forever, together with the thoroughly peaceful life which he had since lived for so many years, had kept up the old man's vitality to a surprising extent. His life was now only fading away by slow and insensible degrees, like the light out of the sunset clouds, or the colors from the mountains — silent warnings of the night coming "in which no man can work."

The minister had worked all his days—his Master's work; none the less worthy that it was done in no public manner, and had met with no public reward. Beyond his own Presbytery the name of the Reverend Alexander Cardross was scarcely known. He was not a popular preacher; he had never published a book, nor even a sermon, and he had taken no part in the theological controversies of the time. He was content to let other men fight about Christianity; he only lived it, spending himself for naught, some might think, in his own country parish and among his poor country people, the pastor and father of them all.

He had never striven after this world's good things,

and they never came to him in any great measure; but better things did. He always had enough, and a little to spare for those who had less. In his old age this righteous man was not "forsaken," and his seed never "begged their bread." His youngest, Duncan, was always beside him, and yearly his four other sons came to visit him from the various places where they had settled themselves, to labor, and prosper, and transmit honorably to another generation the honest name of Cardross.

For the minister's "ae dochter," she was, as she had been always, his right hand, watching him, tending him, helping and guarding him, expending her whole life for him, so as to make him feel as lightly as possible the gradual decay of his own; above all, loving him with a love that made labor easy and trouble light—the passionately devoted love which we often see sons show to mothers, and daughters to fathers, when they have never had the parental ideal broken, nor been left to wander through life in a desolation which is only second to that of being "without God in the world."

"I think he has a happy old age—the dear old father!" said Helen one day, when she and Lord Cairnforth sat talking, while the minister was as usual absorbed in the library—the great Cairnforth library, now becoming notable all over Scotland, of which Mr. Cardross had had the sole arrangement, and every book therein the earl declared he loved as dearly as he did his children.

"Yes, he is certainly happy. And he has had a happy life, too—more so than most people."

"He deserved it. All these seventy-five years he has kept truth on his lips, and honor and honesty in his heart.

He has told no man a lie; has overreached and deceived no man; and, though he was poor—poor always;
when he married my mother, exceedingly poor—he has
literally, from that day to this, 'owed no man any thing
but to love one another.' Oh !" cried Helen, looking after the old man in almost a passion of tenderness, " oh
that my son may grow up like his grandfather! Like
nobody else—only his grandfather."

   " I think he will," answered Lord Cairnforth.

And, in truth, the accounts they had of young Cardross
were for some time extremely satisfactory. He had ac-
commodated himself to his new life—had taken kindly
to his college work; gave no trouble to Mrs. Menteith,
and still less to his uncle; the latter a highly respectable
but not very interesting gentleman—a partner in the firm
of Menteith and Ross, and lately married to the youngest
Miss Menteith.

Still, by his letters, the nephew did not seem over-
whelmingly fond of him, complaining sometimes that
Uncle Alick interfered with him a little too much; in-
vestigated his expenses, made him balance his accounts,
and insisted that these should be kept within the limits
suitable for Mrs. Bruce's son and Mr. Cardross's grandson, who would have to work his way in the world as
his uncles had done before him.

" You see, Helen," said the earl, " all concealment
brings its difficulties. It would be much easier for the
boy if he were told his position and his future career at
once—nay, if he had known it from the first."

·But Helen would not hear of this. She was obstinate,
all but fierce, on the subject. No argument would con-

vince her that it was not safer for her son, who had been
brought up in such Arcadian simplicity, to continue believing himself what he appeared to be, than to be dazzled by the knowledge that he was the chosen heir of
the Earl of Cairnforth.

So, somewhat against his judgment, the earl yielded.

All winter and spring things went on peacefully in the
little peninsula, which was now being grasped tightly by
the strong arm of encroaching civilization. Acre after
acre of moorland disappeared, and became houses, gardens, green-houses, the feu-rents of which made the estate of Cairnforth more valuable every year.

"That young man of yours will have enough on his
hands one day," the earl said to Helen. "He lives an
easy life now, and little thinks what hard work he is
coming to. As Mr. Menteith once told me, the owner
of Cairnforth has no sinecure, nor will have for the next
quarter of a century."

"You expect a busy life, then?"

"Yes; and I must have that boy to help me—till he
comes to his own. But, Helen, after that time, you must
not let him be idle. The richest man should work, if he
can. I wonder what line of work Cardross will take;
whether he will attempt politics—his letters are very po-
litical just now, do you notice?"

"Very. And there is not half enough about himself."

"He might get into Parliament," continued the earl,
"and perhaps some day win a peerage in his own right.
Eh, Helen? Would you like to be mother to a viscount
—Viscount Cairnforth?"

"No," said Helen, tenderly, "there shall never be another Lord Cairnforth."

Thus sat these two, planning by the hour together the
future of the boy who was their one delight. It amused
them through all the winter and spring, till Cairnforth
woods grew green again, and Loch Beg recovered its
smile of sunshiny peace, and the hills at the head of it
took their summer colors, lovely and calm, even as, year
after year, these friends had watched them throughout
their two lives, of which both were now keenly beginning to feel the greater part lay, not before them, but behind. But in thinking of this boy they felt young again,
as if he brought to one the hope, to the other the faint
recollection of happiness that in the great mystery of
Providence to each had been personally denied.

And yet they were not unhappy. Helen was not. No
one could look into her face—strongly marked, but rosy-
complexioned, healthy, and comely — the sort of large
comeliness which belongs to her peculiar type of Scotch
women, especially in their middle age—without seeing
that life was to her not only duty, but enjoyment—ay,
in spite of the widow's cap, which marked her out as one
who permanently belonged and meant to belong only to
her son.

And the earl, though he was getting to look old—older than Helen did — for his black curls were turning
gray, and the worn and withered features, contrasting
with the small, childish figure, gave him a weird sort
of aspect that struck almost painfully at first upon strangers, still Lord Cairnforth preserved the exceeding sweetness and peacefulness of expression which had made his

face so beautiful as a boy, and so winning as a young man.

"He'll ne'er be an auld man," sometimes said the folk about Cairnforth, shaking their heads as they looked after him, and speculating for how many years the feeble body would hold out. Also, perhaps—for self-interest is bound up in the heart of every human being—feeling a little anxiety as to who should come after him, to be lord and ruler over them; perhaps to be less loved, less honored—more so none could possibly be.

It was comfort to those who loved him then, and far more comfort afterward to believe—nay, to know for certain—that many a man, absorbed in the restless struggle of this busy world, prosperous citizen, husband and father, had, on the whole, led a far less happy life than the Earl of Cairnforth.

Chapter the Sixteenth.

ONE mild, sunny autumn day, when Cardross, having ended his first session at college, had spent apparently with extreme enjoyment his first vacation at home, and had just gone back again to Edinburg to commence his second "year," the Earl of Cairnforth drove down to the Manse, as he now did almost daily, for the minister was growing too feeble to come to the Castle very often.

His old pupil found him sitting in the garden, sunning himself in a sheltered nook, backed by a goodly show of China roses and fuchsias, and companioned by two or three volumes of Greek plays, in which, however, he did not read much. He looked up with pleasure at the sound of the wheeled chair along the gravel walk.

"I'm glad you are come," said he. "I'm sorely need-ing somebody, for I have scarcely seen Helen all the morning. There she is! My lassie, where have you been these three hours?"

Helen put off his question in some gentle manner, and took her place beside her charge, or rather between her two charges, each helpless in their way, though the one most helpless once was least so now.

"Helen, something is wrong with you this morning?" said the earl, when, Mr. Cardross having gone away for his little daily walk up and down between the garden and the kirk-yard, they two sat by themselves for a while.

Mrs. Bruce made no answer.

"Nothing can be amiss with your boy, for I had a letter from him only yesterday."

"I had one this morning."

"And what does he say to you? To me little enough, merely complaining how dull he finds Edinburg now, and wishing he were back again among us all."

"I do not wonder," said Helen, in a hard tone, and with that hard expression which sometimes came over her face: the earl knew it well.

"Helen, I am certain something is very wrong with you. Why do you not tell it out to me?"

"Hush! here comes my father!"

And she hurried to him, gave him her arm, and helped his feeble steps back into the house, where for some time they three remained talking together about the little chit-chat of the parish, and the news of the family, in its various ramifications, now extending year by year. Above all, the minister liked to hear and to talk about his eldest and favorite grandchild—his name-child, too—Alexander Cardross Bruce.

But on this subject, usually the never-ceasing topic at the Manse, Helen was for once profoundly silent. Even when her father had dropped asleep, as in his feebleness of age he frequently did in the very midst of conversation, she sat restlessly fingering her wedding-ring, and another which she wore as a sort of guard to it, the only jewel she possessed. It was a very large diamond, set in a plain hoop of gold. The earl had given it to her a few months after she came back to Cairnforth, when her persistent refusal of all his offered kindnesses had almost produced a breach between them—at least the nearest approach to a quarrel they had ever known. She, seeing how deeply she had wounded him, had accepted this ring as a pledge of amity, and had worn it ever since—by his earnest request—until it had become as familiar to her finger as the one beside it. But now she kept looking at it, and taking it off and on with a troubled air.

"I am going to ask you a strange question, Lord Cairnforth—a rude one, if you and I were not such old friends that we do not mind any thing we say to one another."

"Say on."

"Is this ring of mine very valuable?"

"Rather so."

"Worth how much?"

"You certainly are rude, Helen," replied the earl, with a smile. "Well, if you particularly wish to know, I believe it is worth two hundred pounds."

"Two hundred pounds!"

"Was that so alarming? How many times must I suggest that a man may do what he likes with his own? It was mine—that is, my mother's, and I gave it to you. I hope you are worth to me at least two hundred pounds."

But no cheerfulness removed the settled cloud from Mrs. Bruce's face.

"Now—answer me—you know, Helen, you always answer me candidly and truly, what makes you put that question about the ring?"

"Because I wished to sell it."

M

. "Sell it! why?"

"I want money; in fact, I must have money—a good large sum," said Helen, in exceeding agitation. "And as I will neither beg, borrow, nor steal, I must sell something to procure that sum, and this diamond is the only thing I have to sell. Now you comprehend?"

"I think I do," was the grave answer. "My poor Helen!"

She might have held out, but the tenderness of his tone overcame her. She turned her head away.

"Oh, it's bitter, bitter! After all these years!"

"What is bitter? But you need not tell me. I think I can guess. You did not show me your boy's letter of this morning."

"There it is!"

And the poor mother, with her tears fast flowing—they had been restrained so long that now they burst out like a tide—gave way to that heart-break which many a mother has had to endure—the discovery that her son was not the perfect being she had thought him; that he was no better than other women's sons, and equally liable to fall away. Poor Cardross had been doing all sorts of wrong and foolish things, which he had kept to himself as long as he could, as long as he dared, and then had come, in an agony of penitence, and poured out the whole story of his errors and his miseries into his mother's bosom.

They were, happily, only errors, not sins—extravagancies in dress; amusements and dissipations, resulting in serious expenses; but the young fellow had done nothing absolutely wicked. In the strongest manner, and with the most convincing evidence to back it, he protested this, and promised to amend his ways, to "turn over a new leaf," if only his mother would forgive him, and find means to pay the heap of bills which he inclosed, and which amounted to much more than would be covered by his yearly allowance from the earl.

"Poor lad!" said Lord Cairnforth, as he read the letter twice over, and then carefully examined the list of debts it inclosed. "A common story."

"I know that," cried Helen, passionately. "But oh! that it should have happened to *my* son!"

And she bowed her face upon her hands, and swayed herself to and fro in the bitterest grief and humiliation.

The earl regarded her a little while, and then said, gently, "My friend, are you not making for yourself a heavy burden out of a very light matter?"

"A light matter? But you do not see—you can not understand."

"I think I can."

"It is not so much the thing itself—the fact of my son's being so mean, so dishonest as to run into debt, when he knows I hate it—that I have cause to hate it, and to shrink from it as I would from— But this is idle talking. I see you smile. You do not know all the—the dreadful past."

"My dear, I do know—every thing you could tell me —and more."

"Then can not you see what I dread? the first false step—the fatal beginning, of which no one can foresee the end? I must prevent it. I must snatch my poor boy like a brand from the burning. I shall go to Edinburg myself to-morrow. I would start this very day if I could leave my father."

" You can not possibly leave your father," said the earl, gently but decisively. "Sit down, Helen. You must keep quiet."

For she was in a state of excitement such as, since her widowed days, had never been betrayed by Helen Bruce.

" These debts must be paid, and immediately. The bare thought of them nearly drives me wild. But you shall not pay—do not think it," she added, almost fierce-ly. "See what my son himself says—and thank God he had the grace to say it—that I am on no account to go to you; that he 'will turn writer's clerk, or tutor, or any thing, rather than encroach farther on Lord Cairnforth's generosity.'"

" Poor boy! poor boy!"

" Then you don't think him altogether a bad boy ?" appealed Mrs. Bruce, pitifully. " You do not fear that I may live to weep over the day when my son was born?"

The earl smiled, and that quiet, half-amused smile, coming upon her in her excited state, seemed to soothe the mother more than any reasoning could have done.

" No, Helen, I do not think any such thing. I think the lad has been very foolish, and we may have been the same. We kept him in leading-strings too long, and trusted him out of them too suddenly. But as to his be-ing altogether bad — Helen Cardross's son, and the min-ister's grandson—nonsense, my dear."

Mr. Cardross might have heard himself named, for he stirred in his peaceful slumbers, and Helen hastily took her letter from Lord Cairnforth's hand."

"Not a word to him. He is too old. No trouble must ever come near him any more."

"No, Helen. But remember your promise to do nothing till you have talked with me. It is my right, you know. The boy is my boy too. When will you come up to the Castle? To-morrow? Nay, to-night, if you like."

"I will come to-night."

So, at dusk, in the midst of a wild storm, such as in these regions sometimes, nay, almost always succeeds very calm, mild autumn days, Helen appeared at the Castle, and went at once into the library where the earl usually sat. Strange contrast it was between the spacious apartment, with its lofty octagon walls laden with treasures of learning; book-shelves, tier upon tier, reaching to the very roof, which was painted in fresco; every ornamentation of the room being also made as perfect as its owner's fine taste and lavish means could accomplish, and this owner, this master of it all, a diminutive figure, sitting all alone by the vacant fireside—before him a little table, a lamp, and a book. But he was not reading; he was sitting thinking, as he often did now; he said he had read so much in his time that he was rather weary of it, and preferred thinking. Of what? the life he had passed through—still, uneventful, and yet a full and not empty human life? Or it might be, oftener still, upon the life to come?

Lord Cairnforth refused to let his visitor say one word, or even sit down, till he had placed her in Mrs. Campbell's charge, to be dried and reclothed, for she was dripping wet with rain—such rain as comes nowhere but at Loch Beg. By-and-by she reappeared in the library, moving through its heavy shadows, and looking herself again— the calm, dignified woman, "my cousin, Mrs. Bruce," who sometimes appeared among Lord Cairnforth's guests, and whom, though she was too retiring to attract much notice, every body who did notice was sure to approve.

She took her accustomed place by the earl's side, and plunged at once, in Helen's own outspoken way, into the business which had brought her hither.

"I am not come to beg or to borrow, do not think it —only to ask advice. Tell me, what am I to say to my boy?"

And again, the instant she mentioned her son's name, she gave way to tears. Yet all the while her friend saw that she was very hard, and bent upon being hard; that, had Cardross appeared before her at that minute, she would immediately have frozen up again into the stern mother whose confidence had been betrayed, whose principles infringed, and who, though loving her son with all the strength of her heart, could also punish him with all the power of her conscience, even though her heart was breaking with sorrow the while.

"I will give you the best advice I can. But, first, let me have his letter again."

Lord Cairnforth read it slowly over, Mrs. Bruce's eager eyes watching him, and then suffered her to take it from his helpless hands, and fold it up, tenderly, as mothers do.

"What do you think of it?"

"Exactly what I did this morning—that your boy has been very foolish, but not wicked. There is no attempt at deception or untruthfulness."

"No, thank God! Whatever else he is, my son is not a liar. I have prevented or conquered that."

"Yes, because you brought him up, as your father brought us up, to be afraid of nothing, to speak out our minds to him without fear of offending him, to stand in no dread of rousing his anger, but only of grieving his love. And so, you see, Helen, it is the same with your boy. He never attempts to deceive you. He tells out, point-blank, the most foolish things he has done—the most ridiculous expenses he has run into. He may be extravagant, but he is not untruthful. I have no doubt, if I sent this list to his trades-people, they would verify every halfpenny, and that this really is the end of the list. Not such a long list neither, if you consider. Below that two hundred pounds for which you were going to sell my ring."

"Were going! I shall do it still."

"If you will; though it seems a pity to part with a gift of mine, when the sum is a mere nothing to me, with my large income, which, Helen, will one day be all yours."

Helen was silent—a little sorry and ashamed. The earl talked with her till he had succeeded in calming her and bringing her into her natural self again—able to see things in their right proportions, and take just views of all.

"Then you will trust me?" she said at last. "You think I may be depended upon to do nothing rashly when I go to Edinburg to-morrow?"

"My dear, I have no intention of letting you go."

"But some one must go. Something must be done,

and I can not trust Alick to do it. My brother does not
understand my boy," said she, returning to her restless,
helpless manner. She, the helpful Helen, only weak in
this one point—her only son.

"Something has been done. I have already sent for
Cardross. He will be at the Castle to-morrow."

Helen started.

"At the Castle, I said, not the Manse. No, Helen, you
shall not be compromised; you may be as severe as you
like with your son. But he is my son too"—and a faint
shade of color passed over the earl's withered cheeks—
"my adopted son, and it is time that he should know it."

"Do you mean to tell him—"

"I mean to tell him all my intentions concerning him."

"What! now?"

"Yes, now. It is the safest and most direct course,
both for him, for you, and for me. I have been thinking
over the matter all day, and can come to no other conclusion. Even for myself—if I may speak of myself—it is
best. I do not wish to encroach upon his mother's rights
—it is not likely I should," added the earl, with a somewhat sad smile; "still, it is hard that during the years,
few or many, that I have to live, I, a childless man,
should not enjoy a little of the comfort of a son."

Helen sat silent with averted face. It was all quite
true, and yet—

"I will tell you, to make all clear, the position I wish
Cardross to hold with regard to me—shall I?"

Mrs. Bruce assented.

"Into his mother's place he can never step; I do not
desire it. You must still be, as you have always been,

and I shall now publicly give out the fact, my immediate successor; and, except for a stated allowance, to be doubled when he marries, which I hope he will, and early, Cardross must still be dependent upon his mother during her lifetime. Afterward he inherits all. But there is one thing," he continued, seeing that Helen did not speak, "I should like: it would make me happy if, on his coming of age, he would change his name, or add mine to it—be Alexander Cardross Bruce-Montgomerie, or simply Alexander Cardross Montgomerie. Which do you prefer?"

Helen meditated long. Many a change came and went over the widow's face — widowed long enough for time to have softened down all things, and made her remember only the young days — the days of a girl's first love. It might have been so, for she said at last, almost with a gasp,

"I wish my son to be Bruce-Montgomerie."

"Be it so."

After that Lord Cairnforth was long silent.

Helen resumed the conversation by asking if he did not think it dangerous, almost wrong, to tell the boy of this brilliant future immediately after his errors?

"No; not after errors confessed and forsaken. Remember, it was over very rags that the prodigal's father put upon him the purple robe. But our boy is not a prodigal, Helen. I know him well, and I have faith in him, and faith in human nature — especially Cardross nature." And the earl smiled. "Far deeper than any harshness will smite him the consciousness of being forgiven and trusted—of being expected to carry out in his

M 2

future life all that was a-missing in two not particularly
happy lives, his mother's—and mine."

Helen Bruce resisted no more. She could not. She
was a wise woman—a generous and loving-hearted woman; still, in that self-contained, solitary existence, which
had been spent close beside her, yet into the mystery of
which she had never penetrated, and never would penetrate, there was a nearness to heaven and heavenly things,
and a clearness of vision about earthly things which went
far beyond her own. She could not quite comprehend
it—she would never have thought of it herself—but she
dimly felt that the earl's judgment was correct, and that,
strange as his conduct might appear, he was acting after
that large sense of rightness which implies righteousness;
a course of action which the world so often ridicules and
misconstrues, because the point of view is taken from an
altitude not of this world, and the objects regarded there-
from are things not visible, but invisible.

Cardross appeared next day—not at home, but at the
Castle, and was closeted there for several hours with the
earl before he ever saw his mother. When he did—and
it was he who came to her, for she refused to take one
step to go to him—he flung himself on his knees before
her and sobbed in her lap—the great fellow of six feet
high and twenty years old—sobbed and prayed for forgiveness with the humility of a child.

"Oh, mother, mother—and he has forgiven me too!
To think what he has done for me—what he is about to
do—me, who have had no father, or worse than none.
Do you know, sometimes people in Edinburg—the Menteiths, and so on—have taunted me cruelly about my
father?"

"And what do you answer?" asked Helen, in a slow, cold voice.

"That he was my father, and that he was dead; and I bade them speak no more about him."

"That was right, my son."

Then they were silent till Cardross burst out again.

"It is wonderful — wonderful! I can hardly believe it yet—that we should never be poor any more—you, mother, who have gone through so much, and I, who thought I should have to work hard all my days for both of us. And I will work!" cried the boy, as he tossed back his curls and lifted up to his mother a face that in brightness and energy was the very copy of her own, or what hers used to be. "I'll show you, and the earl too, how hard I can work—as hard as if for daily bread. I'll do every thing he wishes me—I'll be his right hand, as he says. I will make a name for myself and him too— mother, you know I am to bear his name?"

"Yes, my boy."

"And I am glad to bear it. I told him so. He shall be proud of me yet, and you too. Oh, mother, mother, I will never vex you again."

And once more his voice broke into sobs, and Helen's too, as she clasped him close, and felt that whatever God had taken away from her, He had given her as much— and more.

Mother and son — widowed mother and only son— there is something in the tie unlike all others in the world—not merely in its blessedness, but in its divine compensations.

Helen waited till her father had retired, which he often

did quite early, for the days were growing too long for him, with whom every one of them was numbered; and he listened to the wonderful news which his grandson told him with the even smile of old age, which nothing now either grieves or surprises.

"You'll not be going to live at the Castle, though, not while I am alive, Helen?" was his first uneasy thought. But his daughter soon quieted it, and saw him to his bed, as she did every evening, bidding him good-night, and kissing his placid brow—placid as a child's—just as if he had been her child instead of her father. Then she took her son's arm—such a stalwart arm now, and walked with him through the bright moonlight, clear as day, to Cairnforth Castle.

When they entered the library they found the earl sitting in his usual place, and engaged in his usual evening occupation, which he sometimes called "the hard labor of doing nothing;" for, though he was busy enough in the daytime with a young man he had as secretary—his faithful old friend, Mr. Mearns, having lately died—still, he generally spent his evenings alone. Malcolm lurked within call, in case he wanted any thing; but he rarely did. Often he would pass hours at a time sitting as now, with his feeble hands folded on his lap, his head bent, and his eyes closed, or else open and looking out straight before him — calmly, but with an infinite yearning in them that would have seemed painful to those who did not know how peaceful his inmost nature was.

But at the first sound of his visitors' footsteps he turned round—that is, he turned his little chair round—and welcomed them heartily and brightly.

A little ordinary talk ensued, in the which Cardross
scarcely joined. The young man was not himself at all
—silent, abstracted; and there was an expression in his
face which almost frightened his mother, so solemn was
it, yet withal so exceedingly sweet.

The earl had been right in his conclusions; he, with
his keen insight into character, had judged Cardross better than the boy's own mother would have done   Those
brilliant prospects, that total change in his expected future, which might have dazzled a lower nature and sent
it all astray, made this boy—Helen's boy, with Helen's
nature strong in him, only the more sensible of his defi-
ciencies as well as his responsibilities—humble, self-dis-
trustful, and full of doubts and fears.   Ten years seemed
to have passed over his head since morning, changing
him from a boy into a sedate, thoughtful man.

Lord Cairnforth noticed this, as he noticed every thing;
and at last, seeing the young heart was too full almost to
bear much talking, he said kindly,

"Cardross, give your mother that arm-chair; she looks
very wearied.   And then, would you mind having a consultation with Malcolm about those salmon-weirs at the
head of Loch Mhor?   I know he is longing to open his
heart to you on the subject.   Go, my boy, and don't hur-
ry back.   I want to have a good long talk with your
mother."

Cardross obeyed.   The two friends looked after him
as he walked down the room with his light, active step,
and graceful, gentlemanly figure—a youth who seemed
born to be heir to all the splendors around him.   Helen
clasped her hands tightly together on her lap, and her

lips moved. She did not speak, but the earl almost seemed to hear the great outcry of the mother's heart going up to God—"Give any thing Thou wilt to me, only give him all!" Alas! that such a cry should ever fall back to earth in the other pitiful moan, "Would God that I had died for thee, O Absalom, my son—my son!"

But it was not to be so with Helen Bruce. Her son was no Absalom. Her days of sorrow were ended.

Lord Cairnforth saw how violently affected she was, and began to talk to her in a commonplace and practical manner about all that he and Cardross had been arranging that morning.

"And I must say that, though he will never shine at college, and probably his grandfather would mourn over him as having no learning, there is an amount of solid sense about the fellow with which I am quite delighted. He is companionable too—knows how to make use of his acquirements. Whatever light he possesses, he will never hide it under a bushel, which is, perhaps, the best qualification for the position that he will one day hold. I have no fear about Cardross. He will be an heir after my own heart—will accomplish all I wished, and possibly a little more."

Mrs. Bruce answered only by tears.

"But there is one thing which he and I have settled between us, subject to your approval, of course. He must go back to college immediately."

"To Edinburg?"

"Do not look so alarmed, Helen. No, not to Edinburg. It is best to break off all associations there—he wishes it himself. He would like to go to a new University—St. Andrew's."

"But he knows nobody there. He would be quite alone. For I can not—do you not see I can not?—leave my father. Oh, it is like being pulled in two," cried Mrs. Bruce, in great distress.

"Be patient, Helen, and hear. We have arranged it all, the boy and I. Next week we are both bound for St. Andrew's."

"You?"

"You think I shall be useless? that it is a man, and not such a creature as I, who ought to take charge of your boy?"

The earl spoke with that deep bitterness which sometimes, though very, very rarely, he betrayed, till he saw what exceeding pain he had given.

"Forgive me, Helen; I know you did not mean that; but it was what I myself often thought until this morning. Now I see that after all I—even I—may be the very best person to go with the boy, because, while keeping a safe watch over him, and a cheerful house always open to him, I shall also give him somebody to take care of. I shall be as much charge to him almost as a woman, and it will be good for him. Do you not perceive this?"

Helen did, clearly enough.

"Besides," continued the earl, "I might, perhaps, like to see the world myself—just once again. At any rate, I shall like to see it through this young man's eyes. He has not told you of our plan yet?"

"Not a word."

"That is well. I like to see he can keep faith. I made him promise not, because I wanted to tell you myself, Helen — I wanted to see how you would take the plan. Will you let us go? That is, the boy must go, and—you will do without me for a year?"

"A whole year! Can not Cardross come home once —just once?"

"Yes, I will manage it so; he shall come, even if I can not," replied the earl, and then was silent.

"And you," said Mrs. Bruce, suddenly, after a long meditation upon her son and his future, "you leave, for a year, your home, your pleasant life here; you change all your pursuits and plans, and give yourself no end of trouble, just to go and watch over my boy, and keep his mother's heart from aching! How can I ever thank you —ever reward you?"

No, she never could.

"It is an ugly word, 'reward;' I don't like it. And, Helen, I thought thanks were long since set aside as unnecessary between you and me."

"'And you will be absent a whole year?"

"Probably, or a little more; for the boy ought to keep two sessions at least; and locomotion is not so easy to me as it is to Cardross. Yes, my dear, you will have to part with me—I mean I shall have to part with you—for a year. It is a long time in our short lives. I would not do it—give myself the pain of it—for any thing in this world except to make Helen happy."

"Thank you; I know that."

But Helen, full of her son and his prospects—her youth renewed in his youth, her life absorbed in his, seeming to stretch out to a future where there was no ending, knew not half of what she thanked him for.

She yielded to all the earl's plans; and after so many years of resistance, bowed her independent spirit to accept his bounty with a humility of gratitude that was almost painful to both, until a few words of his led her to, and left her in the belief that he was doing what was agreeable to himself—that he really did enjoy the idea of a long sojourn at St. Andrew's; and, mother-like, when she was satisfied on this head, she began almost to envy him the blessing of her boy's constant society.

So she agreed to all his plans cheerfully, contentedly, as indeed she had good reason to be contented; thankfully accepted every thing, and never for a moment suspected that she was accepting a sacrifice.

Chapter the Seventeenth.

DURING a whole year the Earl of Cairnforth and Mr. Bruce-Montgomerie—for, as soon as possible, Cardross legally assumed the name—resided at that fairest of ancient cities and pleasantest of Scotch Universities, St. Andrew's.

A few of the older inhabitants may still remember the house the earl occupied there, the society with which he filled it, and the general mode of life carried on by himself and his adopted son. Some may recall—for indeed it was not easy to forget—the impression made in the good old town by the two new-comers when they first appeared in the quiet streets, along the Links and on the West Sands—every where that the little carriage could be drawn. A strange contrast they were—the small figure in the pony-chair, and the tall young man walking beside it in all the vigor, grace, and activity of his blooming youth. Two companions pathetically unlike, and yet always seen together, and evidently associating with one another from pure love.

They lived for some time in considerable seclusion, for the earl's rank and wealth at first acted as a bar to much seeking of his acquaintance among the proud and poor University professors and old-fashioned inhabitants of the city; and Cardross, being the senior of most of the college lads, did not cultivate them much. By degrees, however, he became well known—not as a hard student —that was not his line—he never took any high college honors; but he was the best golfer, the most dashing rider, the boldest swimmer—he saved more than one life on that dangerous shore; and, before the session was half over, he was the most popular youth in the whole University. But he would leave every thing, or give up every thing—both his studies and his pleasures—to sit, patient as a girl, beside the earl's chair, or to follow it— often guiding it himself— up and down St. Andrews' streets; never heeding who looked at him, or what comments were made—as they were sure to be made—upon him, until what was at first so strange and touching a sight grew at last familiar to the whole town.

Of course, very soon all the circumstances of the case came out, probably with many imaginary additions, though the latter never reached the ears of the two concerned. Still, the tale was romantic and pathetic enough to make the earl and his young heir objects of marked interest, and welcome guests in the friendly hospitalities of the place, which hospitalities were gladly requited, for Lord Cairnforth still keenly enjoyed society, and Cardross was at an age when all pleasure is attractive.

People said sometimes, What a lucky fellow was Mr. Bruce - Montgomerie! But they also said — as no one could help seeing and saying—that very few fathers were blessed with a son half so attentive and devoted as this young man was to the Earl of Cairnforth.

And meantime Helen Bruce lived quietly at the Manse, devoting herself to the care of her father, who still lin-

gered on, feeble in body, though retaining most of his
faculties, as though death were unwilling to end a life
which had so much of peace and enjoyment in it to the
very last. When the session was over, Cardross went
home to see his mother and grandfather, and on his return Lord Cairnforth listened eagerly to all the accounts
of Cairnforth, and especially of all that Mrs. Bruce was
doing there; she, as the person most closely acquainted
with the earl's affairs, having been constituted regent in
his absence.

"She's a wonderful woman—my mother," said Cardross, with great admiration. "She has the sense of a
man, and the tact of a woman. She is doing every thing
about the estate almost as cleverly as you would do it
yourself."

"Is she? It is good practice for her," said the earl.
"She will need it soon."

Cardross looked at him. He had never till then noticed, what other people began to notice, how exceedingly old the earl now looked, his small, delicate features
withering up almost like those of an elderly man, though
he was not much past forty.

"You don't mean—oh no, not that! You must not
be thinking of that. My mother's rule at Cairnforth is a
long way off yet." And—big fellow as he was—the lad's
eyes filled with tears.

After that day he refused all holiday excursions in
which Lord Cairnforth could not accompany him. It
was only by great persuasion that he agreed to go for a
week to Edinburg, to revisit his old haunts there, to look
on the ugly fields where he had sown his wild oats, and

prove to even respectable and incredulous Uncle Alick that there was no fear of their ever sprouting up again. Also, Lord Cairnforth took the opportunity to introduce his cousin into his own set of Edinburg friends, to familiarize the young man with the society in which he must shortly take his place, and to hear from them, what he so warmly believed himself, that Cardross was fitted to be heir to any property in all Scotland.

"What a pity," some added, "that he could not be heir to the earldom also!" "No," said others, "better that 'the wee earl' (as old-fashioned folk still sometimes called him) should be the last Earl of Cairnforth."

With the exception of those two visits, during a whole twelvemonth the earl and his adopted son were scarcely parted for a single day. Years afterward, Cardross loved to relate, first to his mother, and then to his children, sometimes with laughter, and again with scarcely repressed tears, many an anecdote of the life they two led together at St. Andrew's—a real student life, yet filled at times with the gayest amusements. For the earl loved gayety—actual mirth; sometimes he and Cardross were as full of jests and pranks as two children, and at other times they held long conversations upon all manner of grave and earnest topics, like equal friends. It was the sort of companionship, free and tender, cheerful and bright, yet with all the influence of the elder over the younger, which, occurring to a young man of Cardross's age and temperament, usually determines his character for life.

Thus, day by day, Helen's son developed and matured, becoming more and more a thorough Cardross, sound to the core, and yet polished outside in a manner which had not been the lot of any of the earlier generation, save the minister. Also, he had a certain winning way with him —a power of suiting himself to every body, and pleasing every body—which even his mother, who only pleased those she loved or those that loved her, had never possessed.

"It's his father's way he has, ye ken," Malcolm would say—Malcolm, who, after a season of passing jealousy, had for years succumbed wholly to his admiration of "Miss Helen's bairn." "But it's the only bit o' the Bruces that the lad's gotten in him, thank the Lord!"

Though the earl did not say openly "thank the Lord," still he, too, recognized with a solemn joy that the qualities he and Helen dreaded had either not been inherited by Captain Bruce's son, or else timely care had rooted them out. And as he gradually relaxed his watch over the young man, and left him more and more to his own guidance, Lord Cairnforth, sitting alone in his house at St. Andrew's—almost as much alone as he used to sit in the Castle library—would think, with a strange consolation, that this year's heavy sacrifice had not been in vain.

Once Cardross, coming in from a long golfing match, broke upon one of these meditative fits, and was a little surprised to find that the earl did not rouse himself out of it quite so readily as was his wont; also that the endless college stories, which he always liked so much to listen to, fell rather blank, and did not meet Lord Cairnforth's hearty laugh, as gay as that of a young fellow who could share and sympathize in them all.

N

"You are not well to-day," suddenly said the lad. "What have you been doing?"

"My usual work—nothing."

"But you have been thinking. What about?" cried Cardross, with the affectionate persistency of one who knew himself a favorite, and looking up in the earl's face with his bright, fond eyes—Helen's very eyes.

"I was thinking of your mother, my boy. You know it is a whole year since I have seen your mother."

"So she said in her last letter, and wondered when you intended coming home, because she misses you more and more every day."

"You, she means, Carr."

"No, yourself. I know my mother wishes you would come home."

"Does she? And so do I. But I should have to leave you alone, my boy; for if once I make the effort, and return to Cairnforth, I know I shall never quit it more."

He spoke earnestly—more so than the occasion seemed to need, and there was a weary look in his eyes which struck his companion.

"Are you afraid to leave me alone, Lord Cairnforth?" asked Cardross, sadly.

"No." And again, as if he had not answered strongly enough, he repeated, "My dear boy, no!"

"Thank you. You never said it, but I knew. You came here for my sake, to take charge of me. You made me happy—you never blamed me—you neither watched men or domineered over me—still, I knew. Oh, how good you have been!"

Lord Cairnforth did not speak for some time, and then he said, gravely,

"However things were at first, you must feel, my boy, that I trust you now entirely, and that you and I are thorough friends—equal friends."

"Not equal. Oh, never in my whole life shall I be half as good as you! But I'll try hard to be as good as I can. And I shall be always beside you. Remember your promise."

This was, that after he came of age, and ended his University career, instead of taking "the grand tour," like most young heirs of the period, Cardross should set-tle down at home, in the character of Lord Cairnforth's private secretary—always at hand, and ready in every possible way to lighten the burden of business which, even as a young man, the earl had found heavy enough, and as an old man he would be unable to bear.

"I shall never be clever, I know that," pleaded the lad, who was learning a touching humility, "but I may be useful; and oh! if you would but use me, in any thing or every thing, I'd work day and night for you— I would indeed!"

"I know you would, my son" (the earl sometimes called him "my son" when they were by themselves), "and so you shall."

That evening Lord Cairnforth dictated to Helen, by her boy's hand, one of his rare letters, telling her that he and Cardross would return home in time for the latter's birthday, which would be in a month from now, and which he wished kept with all the honors customary to the coming of age of an heir of Cairnforth.

"Heir of Cairnforth!"   The lad started, and stopped
writing.

"It must be so, my son; I wish it.   After your moth
er, you are my heir, and I shall honor you as such; afterward you will return here alone, and stay till the session is over; then come back, and live with me at the
Castle, and fit yourself in every way to become—what I
can now wholly trust you to be—the future master of
Cairnforth."

And so, as soon as the earl's letter reached the peninsula, the rejoicings began.   The tenantry knew well
enough who the earl had fixed upon to come after him,
but this was his first public acknowledgment of the fact.
Helen's position, as heiress presumptive, was regarded as
merely nominal; it was her son, the fine young fellow
whom every body knew from his babyhood, toward
whom the loyalty of the little community blazed up in
a height of feudal devotion that was touching to see.
The warm Scotch heart—all the warmer, perhaps, for a
certain narrowness and clannishness, which in its pride
would probably, nay, certainly, have shut itself up against
a stranger or an inferior—opened freely to "Miss Helen's"
son and the minister's grandson, a young man known to
all and approved by all.

So the festivity was planned to be just the earl's coming of age over again, with the difference between June
and December, which removed the feasting-place from
the lawn to the great kitchen of the Castle, and caused
bonfires on the hill-tops to be a very doubtful mode of
jubilation.   The old folk—young then—who remembered the bright summer festival of twenty-four years

ago told many a tale of that day, and how the "puir wee earl" came forward in his little chair and made his brief speech, every word and every promise of which his after life had so faithfully fulfilled.

"The heir's a wise-like lad, and a braw lad," said the old folks of the clachan, patronizingly. "He's no that ill the noo, and he'll aiblins grow better, ye ken; but nae-body that comes after will be like *him.* We'll ne'er see anither Earl o' Cairnforth."

The same words which Mr. Menteith and the rest had said when the earl was born, but with what a different meaning!

Lord Cairnforth came back among his own people amid a transport of welcome. Though he had been long away, Mrs. Bruce and other assistants had carried out his plans and orders so successfully that the estate had not suffered for his absence. In the whole extent of it was now little or no poverty; none like that which, in his youth, had startled Lord Cairnforth into activity upon hearing the story of the old shepherd of Loch Mhor. There was plenty of work, and hands to do it, along the shores of both lochs; new farms had sprung up, and new roads been made; churches and schools were built as occasion required; and though the sheep had been driven a little higher up the mountains, and the deer and grouse fled farther back into the inland moors, still Cairnforth village was a lovely spot, inhabited by a contented community. Civilization could bring to it no evils that were not counteracted by two strong influences — (stronger than any one can conceive who does not understand the peculiarities almost feudal in their simplicity, of country parish life in Scotland)—a minister like Mr. Cardross, and a resident proprietor like the Earl of Cairnforth.

The earl arrived a few days before the festival day, and spent the time in going over his whole property from one end to the other. He took Mrs. Bruce with him. "I can't want you for a day now, Helen," said he, and made her sit beside him in his carriage, which, by dint of various modern appliances, he could now travel in far easier than he used to do, or else asked her to drive him in the old familiar pony-chaise along the old familiar hill-side roads, whence you look down on either loch—sometimes on both—lying like a sheet of silver below.

Many a drive they took every day, the weather being still and calm, as it often is at Cairnforth, by fits and snatches, all winter through.

"I think there never was such a place as this place," the earl would often say, when he stopped at particular points of view, and gazed his fill on every well-known outline of the hills and curve of the lochs, generally ending with a smiling look on the face beside him, equally familiar, which had watched all these things with him for more than thirty years. "Helen, I have had a happy life, or it seems so, looking back upon it. Remember, I said this, and let no one ever say the contrary."

And in all the houses they visited—farm, cottage, or bothie—every body noticed how exceedingly happy the earl looked, how cheerfully he spoke, and how full of interest he was in every thing around him.

"His lordship may live to be an auld man yet," said some one to Malcolm, and Malcolm indignantly repudiated the possibility of any thing else.

The minister was left a little lonely during this week of Lord Cairnforth's coming home, but he did not seem to feel it. He felt nothing very much now except pleasure in the sunshine and the fire, in looking at the outside of his books, now rarely opened, and in watching the bright faces around him. He was made to understand what a grand festival was to be held at Cairnforth, and the earl took especial pains to arrange that the feeble octogenarian should be brought to the Castle without fatigue, and enabled to appear both at the tenants' feast in the kitchen, and the more formal banquet of friends and neighbors in the hall—the grand old dining-room—which was arranged exactly as it had been on the earl's coming of age.

However, there was a difference. Then the board was almost empty, now it was quite full. With a carefulness that at the time Helen almost wondered at, the earl collected about him that day the most brilliant gathering he could invite from all the country round—people of family, rank, and wealth—above all, people of worth; who, either by inherited position, or that high character which is the best possession of all, could confer honor by their presence, and who, since "a man is known by his friends," would be suitable and creditable friends to a young man just entering the world.

And before all these, with Helen sitting as mistress at the foot of the table, and Helen's father at his right hand, the Earl of Cairnforth introduced, in a few simple words, his chosen heir.

"Deliberately chosen," he added; "not merely as being my cousin and my nearest of kin, but because he is his mother's son, and Mr. Cardross's grandson, and worthy of them both—also because, for his own sake, I respect him, and I love him. I give you the health of Alexander Cardross Bruce-Montgomerie.".

And then they all wished the young man joy, and the dining-hall of Cairnforth Castle rang with hearty cheers for Mr. Bruce-Montgomerie.

No more speeches were made, for it was noticed that Lord Cairnforth looked excessively wearied; but he kept his place to the last. Of the many brilliant circles that he had entertained at his hospitable board, none were ever more brilliant than this; none gayer, with the genial, wholesome gayety which the earl, of whom it might truly be said,

> "A merrier man
> I never spent an hour's talk withal,"

knew so well how to scatter around him. By what magic he did this, no one ever quite found out; but it was done, and especially so on this night of all nights, when, after his long absence, he came back to his own ancestral home, and appeared again among his own neighbors and friends. They long remembered it—and him.·

At length the last carriage rolled away, and shortly afterward the wind began suddenly to rise and howl wildly round the Castle. There came on one of those wild winter-storms, common enough in these regions— brief, but fierce while they last.

"You can not go home," said the earl to Mrs. Bruce, who remained with him, the minister having departed with his son Duncan early in the evening. "Stay here till to-morrow. Cardross, persuade your mother. You never yet spent a night under my roof. Helen, will you do it this once? I shall never ask you again."

There was an earnest entreaty in his manner which Helen could not resist; and, hardly knowing why she did it, she consented. Her son went off to his bed, fairly worn out with pleasurable excitement, and she staid with Lord Cairnforth, as he seemed to wish, for another half hour. They sat by the library fire, listening to the rain beating and the wind howling — not continuously, but coming and going in frantic blasts, which seemed like the voices of living creatures borne on its wings.

"Do you mind, Helen, it was just such a night as this when Mr. Menteith died, before I went to Edinburg? The sort of wind that, they say, is always sent to call away souls. I know not why it is, or why there should be any connection between things material and immaterial, comprehensible and wholly incomprehensible, but I often sit here and fancy I should like my soul to be called away in just such a tempest as this—to be set free,

"'And on the wings of mighty winds
Go flying all abroad,'

as the psalm has it. It would be glorious—glorious! suddenly to find one's self strong, active—cumbered with no burden of a body—to be all spirit, and spirit only."

As the earl spoke, his whole face, withered and worn as it was, lighted up and glowed, Helen thought, almost like what one could imagine a disembodied soul.

She answered nothing, for she could find nothing to say. Her quiet, simple faith was almost frightened at the passionate intensity of his, and the nearness with which he seemed to realize the unseen world.

"I wonder," he said again—"I sometimes sit for hours wondering—what the other life is like—the life of which we know nothing, yet which may be so near to us all. I often find myself planning about it in a wild, vague way, what I am to do in it—what God will permit me to do— and to be. Surely something more than He ever permitted here."

"I believe that," said Helen. And after her habit of bringing all things to the one test and the one teaching, she reminded him of the parable of the talents: "I think," she added, "that you will be one of those whom, in requital for having made the most of all his gifts here, He will make 'ruler over ten cities'—at least, if he is a just God."

"He is a just God. In my worst trials I have never doubted that," replied Lord Cairnforth, solemnly. And then he repeated those words of St. Paul, to which many an agonized doubter has clung, as being the last refuge of sorrow—the only key to mysteries which sometimes shake the firmest faith—"'For now we see through a glass darkly, but then face to face; now I know in part, but then shall I know even as also I am known.'"

When Helen rose to retire, which was not till midnight—for the earl seemed unwilling to let her go, saying it was so long since they had had a quiet talk together—he asked her earnestly if she were content about her son.

"Perfectly content. Not merely content, but happy —happier than I once thought it possible to be in this world. And it is you who have done it all—you who have made my boy what he is. But he will reward you

—I know he will. Henceforward he will be as much your son as mine."

"I hope so. And now good-night, my dear."

"Good-night—God bless you."

Mrs. Bruce knelt down beside the chair, and touched with her lips the poor, useless hands.

"Helen," said the earl as she rose, "kiss me—just once —as I remember your doing when I was a boy—a poor, lonely, miserable boy."

She kissed him very tenderly, then went away and left him sitting there in his little chair, opposite the fire, alone in the large, splendid, empty room.

*   *   *   *   *   *

*   *   *   *   *   *

Helen Bruce could not sleep that night. Either the day's excitement had been too much for her, or she was disturbed by the wild winds that went shrieking round the Castle, reminding her over and over again of what the earl had just said concerning them. There came into her mind an uneasy feeling about her father, whom for so many years she had never left a night alone; but it was useless regretting this now. At last, toward morning, the storm gradually lulled. She rose, and looked out of her window on the loch, which glittered in the moonlight like a sea of glass. It reminded her, with an involuntary fancy, of the sea "clear as glass, like unto crystal," spoken of in the fourth chapter of the Apocalypse as being "before the Throne." She stood looking at it for a minute or so, then went back to her bed and slept peacefully till daylight.

She was dressing herself, full of quiet and happy

thoughts, admiring the rosy winter sunrise, and planning all she meant to do that day, when she was startled by Mrs. Campbell, who came suddenly into the room with a face as white and rigid as marble.

"He's awa'," she said, or rather whispered.

"Who is away?" shrieked Helen, thinking at once of her father.

"Whisht!" said the old nurse, catching hold of Mrs. Bruce as she was rushing from the room, and speaking beneath her breath; "whisht! My lord's deid; but we'll no greet; I canna greet. He's gane awa' hame."

No, it was not the old man who was called. Mr. Cardross lived several years after then—lived to be nearly ninety. It was the far younger life—young, and yet how old in suffering!—which had thus suddenly and unexpectedly come to an end.

The earl was found dead in his bed, in his customary attitude of repose, just as Malcolm always placed him, and left him till the morning. His eyes were wide open, so that he could not have died in his sleep. But how, at what hour, or in what manner he had died—whether the summons had been slow or sudden, whether he had tried to call assistance and failed, or whether, calling no one and troubling no one, his fearless soul had passed, and chosen to pass thus solitary unto its God, none ever knew or ever could know, and it was all the same now.

He died as he had lived, quite alone. But it did not seem to have been a painful death, for the expression of his features was peaceful, and they had already settled down into that mysteriously beautiful death-smile which is never seen on any human face but once.

Helen stood and looked down upon it—the dear familiar face, now, in the grandeur of death, suddenly grown
strange. She thought of what they had been talking
about last night concerning the world to come. Now he
knew it all. She did not "greet;" she could not. In
spite of its outward incompleteness, it had been a noble
life—an almost perfect life; and now it was ended. He
had had his desire; his poor helpless body cumbered him
no more—he was "away."

* * * * * *

It was a bright winter morning the day the Earl of
Cairnforth was buried—clear hard frost, and a little snow
—not much—snow never lies long on the shores of Loch
Beg. There was no stately funeral, for it was found that
he had left express orders to the contrary; but four of
his own people, Malcolm Campbell and three more, took
on their shoulders the small coffin, scarcely heavier than
a child's, and bore it tenderly from Cairnforth Castle to
Cairnforth kirk-yard. After it came a long, long train
of silent mourners, as is customary in Scotch funerals.
Such a procession had not been witnessed for centuries
in all this country-side. Ere they left the Castle the funeral prayer was offered up by Mr. Cardross, the last time
the good old minister's voice was ever heard publicly in
his own parish, and at the head of the coffin walked, as
chief mourner, Cardross Bruce-Montgomerie, the earl's
adopted son.

And so, laid beside his father and mother, they left
him to his rest.

According to his own wish, his grave bears this in-
scription, carved upon a plain upright stone, which—also

his particular request—stands with its face toward the unse windows:

Charles Edward Stuart Montgomerie,

THE LAST EARL OF CAIRNFORTH.

DIED · · · · ·

AGED 43 YEARS.

"THY WILL BE DONE ON EARTH AS IT IS IN HEAVEN."

THE END.

Lightning Source UK Ltd.
Milton Keynes UK
UKHW022136190619
344692UK00019B/254/P

9 781103 342181